Chanekka Pullens Publishing Presents

THE SPIRIT BEHIND THE WALL

A Spiritual Revelation of Afro-Americans Freedom

Evg Lael Newlife

Contact Information:

Email: spiritbhwall444@gmail.com

THE SPIRIT BEHIND THE WALL - A Spiritual Revelation of Afro-Americans Freedom

© 2022 Evg Lael Newlife

All Rights Reserved.

Cover art created by Sènami Donoumassou

Edited by Chanekka Pullens

No part of this book may be reproduced or transmitted in any form or by any means, written, electronic, recording, photocopying, or otherwise, without prior written permission of the author, Evg Lael Newlife.

Books may be purchased in quantity by contacting the author by email at: @spiritbhwall444gmail.com , with 'Book Purchase' in the subject line.

ISBN: 978-0-578-29446-9

1. Spiritual   2. History

First Edition

Printed in the USA

Tribute:

- To all the slaves who shed their blood for the abolition of slavery and for the construction of the new world.

- To Martin Luther King Junior, murdered at the age of 39 at Motel Lorraine in Memphis, Tennessee on April 4, 1968.

- To Malcolm X, murdered at the age of 39 in Manhattan, New York on February 21, 1965.

- To Muhammad Ali, who died at the age of 74 in Scottsdale, Arizona on June 3, 2016.

- To President Mathieu Kerekou, former President of the Republic of Benin, who died in Cotonou, Benin at the age of 82 on October 14, 2015.

- To Boubacar Joseph Ndiaye, Curator of the house of slaves on the Island of Gorée in Senegal, who died in Dakar at the age of 86 on February 6, 2009.

Table Of Contents

Introduction 1

The Root 4

The Problem Source 8

The Tree Of Perdition 13

No, To The Continuous Curse 22

Dignity Or Non-Dignity 35

The Spiritual Character Of Slavery 44

The So-Called Successful African Americans 50

Moral And Physical Resolution 57

The Eye Of The Return 62

The Curse Of The Name 76

The Black People's Hidden Value 83

The Bread Of Responsibility 87

The Flip Side Of Slavery In Africa 93

Source 99

A Better Life 106

Conclusion 117

INTRODUCTION

My arrival in the United States of America provoked huge waves of amazement caused by the surprising and very shocking things I witnessed. The reality of the country's black population sent me into a depressed state, in which I stayed until my wife made me realize that such was the way things were here. That I was not hallucinating.

Newly arrived in this country, I was blown away by the gigantism of everything: Washington-Dulles International Airport in Virginia, Sky Phoenix International Airport in Arizona, Thurgood Marshall Baltimore-Washington International Airport of Maryland, Atlanta Savana International Airport, JFK International Airport in New York, Chicago-O'Hare International Airport of Illinois, Dallas/Ford Worth International Airport of Texas. To name but a few. These large airports welcome you with impressive grand roads and imposing buildings. They give you the impression that you are in a country of absolute happiness for all, a country beyond reproach, a country without a stain.

Alas, behind this delusion lies the sad reality: a young black man has just been killed by another black man, a young girl has just lost her virginity at age ten, a fifteen-year-old has just given birth to a baby whose father is unknown and who has no idea what awaits him in the next ten years. Another girl has just been raped or offered to gangs by her mother or father in exchange for drugs to satisfy her or his addiction.

A fourteen-year-old boy has just been sentenced to death or to life imprisonment; another has just been killed by the police for stealing from a supermarket and refusing to comply with the orders of the police officer. A young man in the prime of his life begs for spare change on the sidewalks all day, just so he can buy cigarettes and fast-food meals.

Such a dark depiction can be depressing for anyone who discovers so brutally what black people are going through in their own country. A developed one, offering solutions to less industrialized countries all over the world. I must recover as fast as possible from this depression for I have work to do. Not only to heal the wound in me, but also through my healing, to contribute in my own way to that of those whom I very affectionately call my cousins. African Americans, as they are called today, are descendants of former black slaves. The evil that, in my opinion, has been gnawing at them since the arrival of their forefathers in this land, will come to an end.

This book will not talk about revolt, revolution, or segregation. Nor will it deal with reparation. Its humble ambition is to reach out as a key; to open a door that remained closed in my cousins' lives and keeps them in pain. A spiritual look at an unknown aspect of the realities of their expedition to countries that formerly traded black folks, will surely shed a new light to better understand things. Better yet, make it possible to believe in a reconciliation of their soul and spirit, in order to allow a new beginning and this time around, a real soaring.

This book aims at bringing out the truth that history has refused to confront. It touches the soul and spirit of the black slave. No special solution is needed than to dig into the spiritual aspect of the issues besetting them. I will proclaim the liberation of the inner being of my cousins who have never been in harmony with themselves for eons. Joy will be restored, hope will surely appear as dawn, and ancestral spiritual chains will be untied and broken forever.

The sun rises and sets on a miserable life that does not care about the future. Winter and summer are accomplices of an evil that has never been resolved, but rather reinforced. Years pass, generations follow one another; and there is still no solution to guarantee the future of these youngsters. I look for traces of suffering in order to erase them. I am looking for an origin, so as to wipe the tears of my cousins' souls. Souls that have been weeping for a very long time. I see their gaze turned away from anything that could give hope because it is difficult to reach it. Life is very hard, and there is no plan for the future, but one still has to live. So, one must survive every day.

Tundra, a young woman I met in Washington, D.C., and who lived in Southeast of the nation capital, once expressed to me,

The Spirit Behind The Wall

"*When Africans come to the United States, they have a better life than ours, and think they are better than us. They often say that we, black Americans, are lucky to be born here. Here is what I think: they don't know what they are talking about. We do not know where we come from; it is hard for us to achieve something in this country because we just keep spinning around. We easily betray one another; we can't trust each other; we don't know who we really are. White people first called us negroes, then we became blacks, and nowadays we are told that we are African Americans. They have no idea what to name us. There is neither luck, nor pride in being born in the United States without knowing where one comes from, and what Africa even looks like...*"

CHAPTER I

THE ROOT

I began writing this book after observing the life led by black Americans for a long time. An observation that hurts me and leaves me filled with unanswered questions. In 2007, my first time coming to Washington, D.C., I was stunned to see my cousins in an unpleasant position. For a moment, I thought that the high cost of living in the nation's capital was certainly the cause of this predicament. I compared their situation to that of the people in Africa who abandon the villages and farms to move to the slums of the capital. After visiting some other states (Florida, Virginia, Massachusetts, Illinois, New York, New Jersey, North Carolina, South Carolina, etc.), and looking around the state of Maryland where I am settled; I concluded that my cousins' situation had a different source than I thought. I couldn't figure out how they managed to find themselves facing the same financial challenges, having the same way of talking and dressing, the same way of walking, the same body odor, and the same mentality.

Are their lives similar from one state to another because after all it is the "United States" we are talking about? Each state has its own realities and laws though. Why is it that from New York to Florida, black women raise their children on their own? How come from Maryland to Illinois, young black men are on the streets refusing to go to school? Why is it that from Boston, Massachusetts, to Alexandria, Virginia, the black child hardly ever talks about his father, only his mother? Why are prisons filled with black people from North Carolina to New Jersey? Why do they have to be on the streets from Monday to Sunday not working; but smoking, getting drunk, and doing drugs? Why do my cousins have to stay in the worst living conditions?

This can neither be simply due to a physical cause, nor be a deliberate choice on their part. What does not work in their lives? What did they inherit from their ancestors who were brought to the United States of America for centuries to build the new world? No political, economic, or social reform, offered or fought for, seems to solve their status of exclusion from society.

Citizens on the margins of progress in a developed country, of citizens entirely apart. It seems as if the fate of the slaves still pursues them to this day.

To analyze and really understand this deplorable situation, one must be willing to look beyond the physical realm. No corrective measure of this nature will cure such a profound evil. The cure is to be sought elsewhere. Why not finally probe the metaphysics so dear to their African origins, the world of invisible things? Deportation and distance will not succeed in breaking their umbilical cord. It is, therefore, necessary to finally look for the appropriate answers to the many questions in the spiritual cord that has been operating since their conception. So, we must have a spiritual eye to understand what has really been going on in the lives of African Americans for hundreds of years.

I feel crushed every time I go to black agglomerations. My heart bleeds and my soul weeps from what I see daily on the streets of the United States. Young men and women in unimaginable situations in this era with the world vibrating at an extremely high frequency. That's why it's a necessary start to research and to lay down the parameters dragging this race into negation from generation to generation. Using my spiritual ability, I need to solve the riddle that very few people try to understand. I must find where they've stumbled, like we commonly say in my country. I must find the origin of their suffering and stop it in my own way in order to give a new beginning to the black Americans' future generations.

ORIGINS:

Where do black people come from? My question seems very silly since everyone knows that they all come from Africa. But in reality, black people themselves don't really know where they come from. That is why I asked myself this question as a topic to be studied, as to trace their suffering. This question points us to the history of the African countries that enslaved their daughters and sons. What could lead an individual, a country, a population, a kingdom, to sell his own children to strangers for material things?

What could it be but unawareness, excessive ambition, and a life of illusion which could never be attained? Bitterness stings in my heart because many black Americans today are desperate to know their origins. They can only rely on DNA tests to give them a possible result, through percentages of countries they have come from, particularly West African countries. This seems to provide them with undefined relief.

We even must say that the white slave traders could not know exactly where the slaves they brought back from Africa originated. Those English, Danish, Dutch, French, or Portuguese human traffickers could not identify the countries they got the slaves from. During the slave trade era, Africa was not what it is today. Not countries, but rather kingdoms headed by kings who were powerful rulers and leaders. These kingdoms, simply naïve, were fooled or dominated by white traders in search for strong young people to work in large coffee plantations in the new world. Some kings were so dazzled by exotic gifts that they did not hesitate to offer in exchange, their young and capable children.

Faced with the increasing demand for spices, and therefore the need for slaves, this trade went to a whole new level. Some kingdoms on the West African coast had to wage wars to obtain enough slaves. Among those were the kingdoms on the Atlantic Ocean coast, called the 'Southerners' back home, and who were in direct contact with the European slaves' traders. Young people were captured in the neighboring kingdoms to the north, just as in hunting games. Countries now called Benin, Ghana, Gambia, Nigeria, Senegal, and Togo, etc. fought each other for this inhumane trade.

In Benin, my country of origin and one which was deeply rooted in this trade, there was a very fierce and vigorous kingdom which waged war on all the entities around it. It traveled as far as Nigeria to take slaves. I remember a story that my maternal grandmother told us about her father who had been taken when she was a little girl; he was a Vodou cult high priest, and the king needed him for his slave trade.

In view of the above, we can affirm that black folks in America's origin cannot be defined in relation to a particular country, because slave traders could not actually know it. They can only point to some countries where the slave trade had been intense. I will not defy the DNA tests that are certainly based on lots of research. But I will allow myself, with all due respect to scientists, as a spiritual man and in light of history, to say that a DNA test cannot provide the black Americans with precise details of their origin country. The continent then, was not divided into modern states. Therefore, all that is left to identify their origin is probably the color of their skin, their current living conditions, as well as the stories of the slaves' traders.

As a tribute to the men and women who were victims of the excessive ambition of their brothers and fathers, while respecting their memory, we will answer that they come from the villages of Africa. Villages that have been terrorized and abused, bloodied by an evil trade. The answer will be that they come from far away, from a land they have no memory of. Their origin was erased by the barbarities of their own brothers who did not hesitate to abandon them to endless suffering. They come from a source of a conspiracy between Europeans and their own brothers who were ignorant about the cheap junk they accepted to give them away.

They are simply black folks coming from Africa and will remain black without knowing exactly where they come from.

CHAPTER II

THE PROBLEM SOURCE

Analysis and reflections from the previous chapter, and the answer to all the questions I ask myself, tend to suggest that the sickening situation facing African Americans, or at least its character, is spiritual in terms of how this life of misery is passed down from generation to generation. If so, the curse that plagues them surely stems from somewhere.

The history today tells us truly little of the latter because of their apparent banality. But what could be the harmful effect of these spiritual provisions on black folks in the United States today or elsewhere in the world? Before getting into the surprising spiritual details concerning Benin, I would like to say a few things about this country of which I unveil the fierce methods for delivering its children to infinite suffering.

Throughout my research to find the source of the miserable life led by my black American cousins, an imprint pointed towards Benin in a dream I had as one of the main causes. DAHOMEY was this country's name; the story leading to that name back then proves how merciless the southern DAHOMEAN kings were. Benin is a port country which made it easy for the Europeans to access it by the Atlantic Ocean. Its neighbors are Burkina Faso in the northwest, Niger in the northeast, Nigeria in the east, and Togo in the west. According to history, the slave traders first docked in Dahomey in the 15th century, and the country quickly became a main exit door for slaves in Africa. Recognized worldwide as a powerful supplier of slaves through Ouidah, one of its coastal cities, Benin is the cradle of Vodou, and many deities are worshipped; the first religions in this country before the arrival of Christianity and Islam.

Our interest in this country is the Vodou rituals, which was then a tool used in the slave trade. It could be a source of the problems my black American cousins are experiencing today. Vodou is the worship of entities and spirits to which the inhabitants of this country, especially in the south, are dedicated. He represents their "God". Vodou is many Divinities which have representations and temples of worship where many animal sacrifices are made for the maintenance of the deities. So, when this occult tradition of Vodou is linked to slavery, it means the practices back in time, as well as today, nothing can be done without consulting the fetishes. This explains the direct involvement of this practice in the human trade; humans who must first be captured. So, after the fetishes were consulted, many occult rituals were conducted in order to ensure that capturing the slaves and sending them off, happened without a glitch. As I mentioned earlier, some kings went to war to have enough slaves to sell, and these wars were not done without consulting the various gods to see whether they would win or lose in the operation. It should also be noted that capturing slaves was similar to going hunting.

The hunters were well equipped with defenses and weakening measures to control the slave until he was sold to the Europeans. Many occult practices were implemented to successfully wage the various wars the kingdoms involved in this trade were conducting against one another, and to facilitate the capture of slaves. I would like to demonstrate here that these occult Vodou practices had a tremendous effect on the souls of the slaves before and after they were sold. Sets of amulets usually called "GRIGRIS" as well as incantatory words were used. It is known that in Vodou these incantatory words and amulets are not vain instruments. They are immensely powerful and can have a profound impact on the spirits of the victims; to the point of affecting everyone over several generations.

In this context, one should easily understand that the incantatory words that were spoken could never be blessings to the slaves. But rather occult and powerful proclamations intended to weaken them in order to dominate them physically and mentally. The spiritual manipulations to which slaves were subjected from the beginning of their long adventure indicated the misfortune awaiting them, and that they were automatically surrendered to the spirit of bondage. The very first condemnation the slaves were subjected to came from the transformation of their human spirit into a spirit of servitude. The latter, in which was instilled into them as soon as they were captured, defined their fate and their status as condemned for the rest of their lives.

To further illustrate this real possibility of spiritual communication between master and captured, here is an example: There is an ethnic group in northern Benin, and most West African countries called Fulani. They are nomads and shepherds of oxen and sheep. These nomadic people have the art of communicating directly with their herd. This ability leaves no one indifferent because no one knows the language they use. When the Fulani shepherd sells an animal of his flock, he must speak to it as if he were giving the animal firm advice or instructions about his new master.

At my grandmother's funeral, we went to my village to buy an ox, but the tempestuous ox refused to get into the van to be transported. The animal was so enraged, no one dared approach him. So, we went to look for a Fulani shepherd in his camp a little further from our village. When he arrived, he approached the animal uttering a simple word from afar, he struck the animal's back three times, spoke in his ears, and invited us to put him in the van. The animal that was furious earlier became all obedient, cooperative, and totally different from the one we had seen a few minutes prior. The ox got into the van without much effort on our part and quietly laid down until he was killed. It was as if the Fulani shepherd had said to this animal, *"This is your new fate, you just have to accept it, there is nothing else to do."* Or something else like, *"My dear friend, Ox, you only have one option here: it's to set your fury aside and accept your fate."* This has nothing in common with what we see in the familiar relationship between a dog and his owner. Our helper that day was not that ox's owner, it was just a random shepherd whom we went to for help.

This story is a perfect illustration which demonstrates that Africa possesses mystical powers of weakening and controlling a mind just through words, but not just merely any words. If one went capturing human beings just as one went hunting, it clearly indicates that they were not perceived as humans. But rather, they were considered animals, such as oxen, bulls, or wild donkeys that could be captured, tamed, and sold to work in farms; the slaves were dehumanized. Therefore, every means was used for the human hunting business because the prey were not merely animals, but two-legged animals who were similar to the hunters themselves. These occult means and incantatory condemning words were then used as ruthless reinforcements to dictate their new fate to the slaves as the Fulani had done to the furious ox.

The conversion of the slaves from human beings to animals constitutes a second condemnation. These men and women's fate were sealed with incantatory discharges which they had no choice but to accept; for there was this physical and spiritual power imposed on them when they were captured. They were automatically condemned to this slave spell, and the spirit of bondage settled in them. It accompanied them to the United States, the American continents, and other countries around the world.

The spirit of the slave or bondage did not leave them after slavery ended. On the contrary, it created other spells, killings, injustices, and horrible actions coming from certain groups of white folks. These groups organized themselves to eradicate the black race who were freed from their physical hold. The spirit of bondage continues to operate in the lives of the descendants of these slaves to this day. That is why they cannot understand the life they lead.

This state of alienation must be revealed to the innocent descendants who share the same fate. Someone must create the awareness in them about it, and that is the fundamental reason for this book. Black people in the United States probably still have a long way to go, according to what I have witnessed since my arrival in this country. Even those who have resettled in the Caribbean, Haiti, Liberia, or elsewhere in the world, still carry the curses of the unknown origin. They cannot hope to become masters of this country under these circumstances. Many of them lack direction in their lives and are spiritually and mentally confronted with a multiple personality issue. The situation experienced by African Americans causes sadness and inspires a real desire to do something to save future generations from this fate. My heart bleeds, and my soul cries because everything I see with my spiritual eyes demonstrates that ancestral suffering is not recognized by those who used them and is not beneficial to future generations.

Here, I am talking about what I know of the history of Benin, my country of origin. I only put an emphasis on the aspects which concern its great responsibility through the Vodou practice in this human trafficking. Africa was not a Christian or Muslim Africa in the beginning. These religions came to find out that Africa was already practicing Vodou. This book only talks about what I know and what is supported by evidence. That is why I am focusing on my country, which has played a central role in the spiritual trade. However, this cannot be only limited to my country. History tells us that of the approximate eleven million slaves taken from Africa, just over two million left Benin. So, why do we see profound suffering in the lives of the people we are talking about? Why are they carrying the same curses to this day? Why do their lifestyles remain the same?

Based on my knowledge of the West African coast, all the countries that have been affected by this vile trade are Vodou practitioners, with the possible exception of Gambia and Senegal which served more as shipping hubs. It is true that Benin is pointed at as the cradle of the practice of Vodou; but many other countries like Ghana, Nigeria, and Togo cannot be left out. Africa cannot deny Vodou, especially the southern populations of the countries mentioned above.

What then were the occult arrangements that neighboring countries to Benin made in connection with the slaves' trade? Even though I can't really give details, I can affirm that they couldn't have operated differently since groups of slaves who, under the same conditions, left on their side too without ever coming back to this day. This curse is distributed among black Americans like contagion; more than 80% of this group of people in the United States of America is affected.

Hearts will be deeply saddened, because we must denounce everything that encompasses their situation; revealing how these things happened and why they were imposed on them. I will do my best to reveal this, in the interest of my readers, by highlighting some details that would help to limit the shocks. This book is intended to be a great revelation that will help steer the black race towards its spiritual liberation.

CHAPTER III

THE TREE OF PERDITION

THE TREE OF FORGETFULNESS (Ouidah, Benin)

I am only talking about what I know and can prove. That is why I base my story on my country's history, and the conclusion I draw from this history, through the landmarks left by the ancestors who sold the slaves. Today, however, there is a historical reference that defines the sale of slaves that took place some centuries back. The circuit of slavery is defined by many very touching stages as recounted by our historians in Benin. According to what we have studied, and which is officially recognized, there is a historical trail that has been called the "Slave Route". Instead of repeating the same things my elders have already said, my goal is to demonstrate the occult spiritual aspect that is often gone unnoticed in the stories that are told.

The focus from the beginning of the book has been on the spiritual aspect of our topic. A particular fetish tree which was an essential instrument in the slave trade program in Benin, then Dahomey, was planted.

Around 1727, a few years after the European slave traders set foot on the shores of Benin, mainly in the village of Guéléwé, now called Ouidah, an important arrangement was made under the reign of a fierce king named AGADJA. The fetish tree was to be planted with the agenda of protecting and helping sellers to lead the slave trade without fear. This fetish tree, endowed with an occult power by the Vodou, was established to train the slaves in another physical and spiritual dimension. It offered complete satisfaction and assurance of what they were doing to their captured brothers. The fetish tree I'm referencing is no secret for some who have already visited the Slave Route in Benin. It is called the tree of oblivion/ forgetfulness, and in my view, is one of the main causes for my cousins' unfortunate situation today.

I am deeply bothered by the characters of this tree, planted by human beings against their own brothers just to get junk from strangers. I am beset by inexplicable headaches every time I study the spiritual aspect of the tree of oblivion.

When I connect spiritually to analyze this tree in depth, I experience odd sensations as if I should not talk about it. It took me two months of spiritual relaxation before writing this chapter. When we go into the spiritual details, we see that everything has been played on the lives of my black American cousins from this very powerful fetish tree.

King AGADJA, during his reign, had initiated with Vodou high priests the fetish tree to make security arrangements for his kingdom. In fact, no one knew the destination of the sold slaves. No one could say how far they were going, and it could be a huge problem if one of them ever came back. The slaves had no idea where they were going. They only knew that they were going to the ocean and could not guarantee that they would return. Because of that reason, a security provision was needed, which guaranteed the king and the traders that they would never return to the kingdom. They were well aware of the abuse that they were inflicting their own brothers to before they left. Especially of the harm they were doing by selling them to white folks who came from an unknown land.

The fetish tree had a well-defined function; to completely erase the memory of the slave. It played the role of formatting software as in a computer. The slave was to forget his origin, his identity, through the effect of that tree. What's more upsetting is while during my research on this tree, I discovered that on top of stripping the slaves of all their landmarks and values, it transformed them into an animal state. It is easy for stories today to speak of this tree as a symbol, but I must confess that the spiritual aspect of this tree is nothing simple and negligible. It mainly explains what we see today in the United States and elsewhere in the lives of the descendants of slaves. They were simply stripped of their identity, their personality. The character I am bringing out of this fetish tree is the state in which they left their homes. They no longer had any knowledge of their origin or identity. The occult power was used, in my viewpoint, to lock their subconscious in the tree.

How can we explain that a simple tree can erase an individual's memory, if it is not mystical? To achieve this result, Vodou Priests initiated a practice according to the gender of the individual. Circling the tree a certain number of times took away the individual's mental abilities. Numbers nine and seven were the spiritual values of the tricks to be done to obtain a proper result of this tree.

The male slaves circled the tree nine times because they have nine ribs, and the female seven times because they have seven ribs. The result was perfect. Even though science says something else today about the human's ribs, I believe that the ancestors had a spiritual definition of things. The numbers nine and seven in the spiritual have a well-defined position in occult practices. Circling around the fetish tree nine or seven times were imprints of spiritual resolve, leading the slaves to be devoid of any identity, and any reason that could make them return to their homeland.

Many questions arise about the fetish tree, so I tried to find out what it was made of. I couldn't obtain any details because these rituals are considered top spiritual secrets. I was able to collect bits and pieces of information from a few priests; information that allowed me to have an idea of the foundation of this fetish. Certain ingredients, that I cannot list here because they were not revealed to me, are necessary in order to establish such an occult arrangement. According to various Vodou Priests interviewed and following the time's well-known practices, elements such as the head of a mad person or a living human being, a living antelope, or a living lion, etc. had to be buried first at the precise location the fetish tree would be planted.

That was a powerful spiritual mechanism that could easily imprison the slaves' memory and identity. In conclusion, the fetish tree was simply an occult arrangement to ensure that the sold cousins never returned to their homeland. The tree of oblivion was a fetish for sending slaves into complete forgetfulness; because someone who no longer has any memory or reference, someone who has been transformed from a human being into an animal, has completely lost his tracks. He has been stripped of all his senses and is, therefore, in darkness.

Let us pause at this point to silence our mind and go into a meditative state. The goal here is to understand and experience, in a few seconds, the state in which the slaves who left the coast of Benin had arrived in the United States. Relax, breathe deeply, put yourself in a state of receptivity, and let go for just a few seconds; connect with nature; feel the presence and effects of the tree of oblivion. You should either feel warm from your head to your feet via your whole body or cool from the soles of your feet with chills. Stop! Stop! Stop! Don't go any further this is very powerful. A spirit does not die; he keeps all the sacrifices that have been offered to him and any data communicated with him. The fetish is still very much alive and real, even though it is difficult to find its real spot in Ouidah today. It is still active in the lives of black Americans in the United States who are experiencing the aftermath effects such as the lack of identity and personality.

Nowadays, the tree of oblivion is invisible to the population of Ouidah. Vodou Priests are well aware of its value and its effects. They can communicate with it provided they have the permission of the deceased ancestors; Vodou Priests in the invisible world. The invisibility of the tree is somehow intriguing though. It's a wonder why it had to disappear in the eyes of the inhabitants of the city. However, there are still some trees in Ouidah that are more than two hundred years old and belong to the Vodou order. I know at least the story of a tree in the sacred forest in Ouidah which grows in the opposite direction of other trees, with its roots in the air and its leaves on the ground. The Late Jean Pliya, who was a renown spiritual being and writer, had also demonstrated in his book, *The Fetish Tree*, the power and occult characters of trees in Benin. This demonstrates the existence of the so-called fetish trees in Benin. Does the tree of oblivion no longer exist to be venerated like other Divinities? Let's just say that because of the dangerous nature of the tree, the ancestors could not leave such an instrument as a legacy to their descendants. The tree of oblivion was used to harm people who were to be taken away from the land of their forefathers.

The lack of truth can cause confusion in our lives. Today, the revelation of the tree of oblivion is to help my African American cousins; to help them find a path which has been lost since their ancestors.

The cousins to whom I pay tribute in this book arrived in the United States in an animal state. They have mostly left their identity, their culture, and the memory of their origin in the tree of oblivion. That arrangement could only be a curse for all black folks whose ancestors have passed through the fetish tree. This curse has not been broken yet and isn't going to be. I now understand the deep reasons for the reality my cousins face here.

One can never be free if spiritual arrangements have been made for one's ancestral identity to be erased. The English, Dutch, Danish, French, and Portuguese slave traders were simple merchants who sold humans beings. They were not Vodou Priests. But those who sold their brothers were the fetish masters who made the occult arrangements. I have always heard in my country that Vodou was at the service of man; they used it to hurt their brothers, giving them no chance to physically return to their homeland. They gave their brothers no chance to defend themselves in the ships which transported them. They gave them no chance.

Today, we should see the slaves' history differently. We should look at it through a spiritual lens and understand the black children living in precarious conditions today. Centuries has passed, but the fetish tree's effects are still noticeable. The Afro-Americans' lack of identity and personality can be rooted in the mark of the tree. The animosity black folks show each other, the betrayal for vain things, the remorseless murder of those who could help them get by, demonstrate the animal state to which the tree of oblivion had reduced their ancestors.

They were marked as animals, recognized, and treated as such from the beginning, following the obligatory passage by the tree of oblivion. They have been defined as 'savages' from Africa. They were carriers of AKOKO, which was the same yoke that carried the bulls of the fields. Even though the 'AKOKO' has been removed by the 13th Amendment of the Constitution of the United States of America, its effects are still being felt in black communities. There is neither a compass nor an orientation, and generation after generation the same problems and stories repeats perpetually.

The Spirit Behind The Wall

Loann _ Farhan

The image of the spirit of the tree of forgetfulness around which slaves should turn seven or nine times depending on their sex to completely forget their identity and their origin. It is located in Ouidah, Republic of Benin.

THE LAST BATH (DONKO NSUO River in Ghana):

I've always wondered about the real reasons behind the bath that slaves were forced to take before they were delivered. A river, like a tree, can be of a sacred nature in the African culture. Culturally and mystically, Benin and Ghana have similar Vodou practices, and those practices are common in the south of both countries. There are also Divinities in Benin that were inherited from Ghana via Togo. Make note that the arrangements made by our ancestors cannot be taken lightly. So, what exactly did that last bath taken by the slaves mean? We have already established that nothing good happened to the captured slaves. Even though history tells us that slaves washed up before they were sold as to increase their market value, I see this mandatory bath as something completely different.

A river, as I mentioned earlier, is sacred and could be of two dimensions: either to condemn or to purify. Why this mandatory bath? Having understood that the person selling his brothers couldn't hold any good intention towards the latter, I can conclude that, the last bath was neither a refreshing one, nor a purification one. It was certainly a goodbye bath. They said goodbye to the ancestors' land forever the minute they got out of that river. They had nothing to expect from their homeland after that bath. It was a separation bath, in my opinion, and it hurts when you put yourself in the slaves' shoes. Imagine yourself taking one last bath knowing you will never again set foot in your place of origin, your birthplace, that you will never return home. Feel the sensations felt by the one who knew he was leaving forever, and that he was bathing for the last time in the place which was his world.

It's like bathing a dead person for the last time before burying them. One felt moved, touched, sad, and disgusted all at once thinking that they were saying goodbye forever to their land of origin. The river took something from them and left something in them. It should be named the river of bitterness, the river of no return, the river of oblivion. They left everything behind in this river that kept their memory and value. Their heritage, their human values were swallowed by a bath; the slave lived by what he was told he was. They left this water without taking anything from their origin. Africans, in general, let the chicken drink before killing it. This act is very symbolic. In this context, their last act was to refresh their souls, and make them seal their departure without the possibility of a return. The Donko Nsuo River in Ghana and the tree of oblivion in Benin were instruments to make sure that slaves, as well as their descendants, would be lost and never returned until further spiritual order.

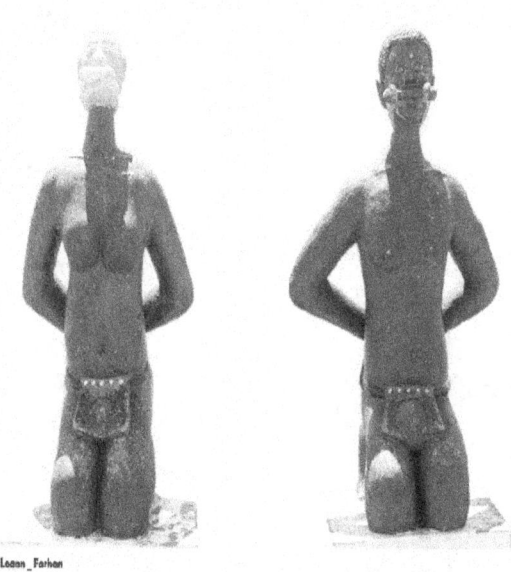

Loann_Farhan

After the transformation of the tree of forgetfulness, the communication with the slave will be made through what the Moors called **"Akoko"**. *This image is the statuettes of female and male slaves carrying the Akoko in their mouths.*

CHAPTER IV

NO, TO THE CONTINUOUS CURSE

I feel like it is imperative to find a solution to the negative parameters affecting my cousins by choosing the therapeutic path. I am doing so to appeal to their conscience and to find a way to reverse the curse that has been plaguing them for centuries.

I consider **X** the element which will represent the solution to the evil. The mathematical formula is: $(-) \times (-) = +$. The **X** in the middle of the two negatives is not only the multiplier, but another well-defined operation which will cause both negatives to give the positive. I call **X** "SPIRITUAL THERAPEUTIC OPERATION".

In the book, *The Power of I Am,* Joel Osteen declares, *"If you're going to go to the next level, you have to say so."* In his book, he demonstrated the power of speaking into existence something that already exists in the spiritual world. *"Nothing happens until one speak,"* he reveals. My opinion concurs with his declaration. We must speak to materialize the evil plaguing our lives by verbalizing it in order it to find the definitive solution. We would thus have to verbalize them to proceed to the operation **X**, SPIRITUAL THERAPEUTIC.

What does this mean in this particular context? Being aware that this curse eats away in silence and is not revealed. It would be important for us to recognize it and acknowledge its presence. It is important to know that this evil exists, to recognize its disrepute in one's life in order to take steps to end it.

Here is an example of my elder sister who was regularly involved in car accidents, to the point that her car insurance skyrocketed. At her last accident, she was given a warning that if she was in any of those inexplainable accidents again in the next three years, her driver's license will be suspended for five years. At that point it was important to find a solution to stop that pattern once and for all.

We had to stir our brains, look at the situation through a spiritual eye, and above all, trace my sister's repeated accidents, finding their invisible and spiritual source. As it turned out the problem originated from our father's house. Our father had always been involved in repeated accidents on motorbikes, cars, and even in a plane once if my memory serves me correctly. But the good thing about all this is that he always walked away with scratches and sometimes nothing. There were sometimes deaths in some of the accidents that he was involved in. So, the source of my sister's repeated accidents was of a spiritual nature, and we had to bring this invisible source to the surface and put an end to it. Where in this story are the two negatives and **X** the operation to be performed?

The first negative **(-)** is the origin of the accidents, the source of the accident that has plagued our family for years.

The second negative **(-)** is the materialization of the evil into the physical by seeking what is wrong and defining it.

For the operation **X**, it is now important to start from the rejection of the evil and to carry out spiritual exercises to end it forever. The accidents have since then miraculously disappeared from my sister's life, and I can assure you that there will be no more, because the source has been destroyed at her level.

This applies to all our lives one way or another. Simply acknowledging a truth frees us, and makes the evil contained in it lose its disastrous hold on our lives when exposed. I, myself had to go through the same process to deal with a personal problem. It was not easy for me to defeat it. That evil kept me awake at night and caused me countless enemies. In my case, I did not accept criticism. I did not appreciate people making comments about my mistakes or the mistakes I could make. I preferred dealing with my mistakes later, rather than someone noticing earlier and telling me about them. To me, it was as if I was in a position of weakness. I did not want anyone finding out about my vulnerability. I spent most of my time working rather than having to ask someone for help. That situation ate away at me; and I preferred it that way. Just to prove to those who, since my childhood, said that I will not amount to anything that they were wrong.

I nurtured pride ever since I was a child because of the belief system I have been exposed to. Pride with which I lived with for a long time, until the night my wife sat me down, and brought the subject up for more than two hours. My first reaction was to try to end the conversation, but I felt so helpless inside, I could not even utter a word. I was like a little boy attentively listening to his mother. My wife had verbalized the foundation on which my life was based, she exposed the real me. She wanted my life to move to a superior level, so she had to talk about this thing which was hidden in me. She didn't just stop there though, she helped me proceed to the operation **X** by accepting the truth, materializing it, and finally wiping it out of my system. I accomplished this by taking actions contrary to the ones I usually took, with prayer and meditation. It was not easy in my case, but I managed to put an end to this lifelong situation. I am cured of that internal problem, which prevented me from humbling myself. I used to be a boy who just wanted to be left alone in his corner. Who did not hesitate to say what he thought directly into the face of whomever came to him. I was inwardly tough.

I had to rewrite this book in order to review everything I had denounced in it as I might have been under the influence of my former personality. My first draft was shocking as I was told, but I did not see it that way. To me, my Afro-American cousins brought their infortunes upon themselves because they did not take the bulls by the horns. Thanks to my wife, who performed the therapeutic operation in my life, the ailment I have dragged around for years is cured. That helped me revisit the book and use a softer tone. I remember her telling me, *"You can't help your cousins if you don't heal yourself first, because your heart bleeds for what you see. And I feel the bitterness, the pain that provokes the violent anger in what you wrote. For you to help your cousins, you must do so from a place of love, not of anger or war."* In a nutshell, writing this book healed me from an issue I carried around for over thirty years; a problem, I inherited from my father, who to this day is unable to humble himself even though it bothers him.

$(-) \times (-) = +$; the first negative $(-)$ is the source of the problem, the evil on the spiritual plane.

The second negative $(-)$ is the materialization of the problem, its recognition on the physical plane.

X is the spiritual therapeutic operation; and the **+** is the positive result. I am prouder of my book after the therapeutic work on myself that lasted at least three months. I know that the path to liberation has been found for my black American cousins.

Everything I talk about in this chapter is for a purely therapeutic purpose. It is not for criticism or reproach of any kind with the intention of harming anyone. I'm helping in understanding the origin of the problem and confirming its existence in my cousins' lives. It is, therefore, important to look with love in order to understand what is going on in your life. I would recommend to everybody, black and white alike, but especially to my cousins, in case they recognize one of the four points I will list, to simply take it as a revelation and seek to materialize this point so as to proceed with spiritual therapeutic operation **X**.

Four main points emerge from all the practices used to transform the minds of the slaves before sending them to an unknown land. Non-identity, violence, personality confusion, and perdition are the four essential points which could mark the horrific use of the fetish tree in the lives of slaves. Occult practices had not been initiated to benefit the slaves in any way, but rather to negatively impact their lives before they were sold and transported to Europe and America in total darkness. I am revising things to better bring out the true meaning of the curse that has been going on for centuries and has remained unresolved. Slavery history continues to make white folks rich, if I may say so, but keeps blacks in poverty and suffering. Black folks, whether they sold their brothers or were sold, are always poor. Most of them live in an unspeakable misery and this can only be defined as a curse.

The slave trade could have made sense if Benin, Ghana, or any other African country that participated in it, had been able to derive a substantial gain from it. Unfortunately, none of those countries has become wealthy or developed by selling its own children. Nobody goes into business to lose, as far as I know, but to earn and have an independent life. How could human trade be profitable to any country selling its own children? I could understand the reasons for this trade if my country did not continue accepting junk, and worse, reaching out to these same buyers, in exchange for the blood of its children since slavery was abolished.

Slavery must, therefore, be marked as a curse for both the seller and the slaves. What good did erasing the slaves' memory and stripping them of their human value do? Absolutely none! All the fetish tree, river, and any occult ritual observed caused was despair and ongoing suffering. Even so today in Africa, Benin, Ghana, etc., for the traders as well as the slaves' descendants.

A fetish has principles and executes orders of the Vodou Priest according to these principles. A fetish works in the sense of a contract and produces results in compliance with this contract. Now, where is the fetish tree today? Where is this tree in the city of Ouidah? No one can say for sure. Did our ancestors fortuitously abandon it? Or did they cut it to make it disappeared from the eyes of future generations because of its powerful identity-destroying characteristics? Why didn't anybody tell me about the composition of this brain and subconscious formatting fetish? During my research, it was reported to me that the Vodou dignitaries, the class of the Vodou order in Ouidah, are consulting to embark on the traces of the tree of oblivion. They are doing so to find its true dwelling and relocate it. This scares me for my people. We know that the tree has brought lots of misfortune to our Afro-American cousins, and even to the descendants of the tree's initiators. None of them are living a happy life.

Today, when you go to Ouidah, the tour guides take you to a mermaid statue facing the ocean with a trumpet in her mouth. This statue supposedly represents the tree of oblivion, until further spiritual order. Nothing is done for nothing in the occult world. Why a mermaid statue? I have no answer to that question. But I do know that the mermaid is the MAMIWATA (Mummy Water), which in Benin is a goddess of waters that a group of people worships. This Vodou worship circle came from Ghana. So, in my opinion, there may be a relationship between the tree and the spirits of the waters. This allows me to link the tree of oblivion to the river of the last bath of Ghana.

Water is an element that erases and cleans. Were the spirits of the waters the source of this tree? Was the memory of the slaves transported into the ocean to be drowned or preserved in the sea as was done in Ghana across the Donko Nsuo River? This point is very deep. It should be noted that the tree of oblivion has left its marks on black folks' lives just like this river; and they still deeply suffer from it.

A while ago, I discussed black life issues with a young white student whom I had the opportunity to transport to Washington, D.C. National Airport (DCA). She told me that African Americans' life difficulties are a huge problem for the United States. I replied that this will remain the case as long as the arrangements that were made before their expedition to America are not corrected. They came to America not in their normal state of mind, but in a spiritual state that suited those who used them. Now, it has become a problem for them. Evil is there for all Americans. It's human blood we are talking about; human beings transformed so they could be manipulated by traffickers. Slaves who no longer had all their mental faculty at their time of arrival here. Those actions have enormous repercussions, and the descendants on both sides will suffer the consequences in their own way.

The tree we are talking about had received promises before going into operation mode. Why do we have to find it? The tree of oblivion is heard of today through my book. It is rather regrettable that the descendants who have nothing to do with this sad past, are now paying the high price by suffering from this curse.

The four points that characterize the aspect of the curse to which we must all say, *"NO!"*, has a spiritual source. It reflects the way in which the slaves were prepared before being delivered to the traders. So, we need to relive these points to: get their true meaning, better understand the experiences of African Americans in the past, as well as today, and also implement an important spiritual support for the future generations.

The absence of identity: One's identity refers to memories, relationships, values, and experiences from birth and is one's point of support as to who one is. It presents one with a future that one can believe in to make one's life. If one's identity is absent and/or neutralized by various physical or spiritual means, one can no longer be considered a full human being. Occult practices through the tree, and other means, has helped snatch the slaves' bearings from their lives. It can be insinuated that their identity is spiritually absent. The fetish tree took the slaves' physical-spiritual data that would have been in his subconscious, and which could have provided him with references.

Are there still black folks without identity? I'll say, *"Yes!"* Observing their reaction reveals an absence of identity which they seek by different means.

I will often come back to this aspect of lack of identity, which is one of the sources of black folks' problems. They have no idea who they are really and have no way of knowing it since their ancestors didn't know who they were either. As such, they couldn't leave a source or reference of their identity to their descendants. The slaves' souls have no reference, so they are souls lost inside physical bodies. The slaves' descendants just go through the motions living with no purpose. Identity is imperative because without it, one can build nothing.

There is a slave group called "Bula" in South Carolina; they were brought from Sierra Leone. Slaves from this ethnic group were able to find their origins in West Africa and trace their culture. Today, there are even restaurants which have Bula menus. This means that those slaves came to America with some sense and their identity intact which they were able to transfer to their offspring. Descendants from that slave group know where they come from and can even speak the Bula language in their own way. We've observed that this group of former slaves are more or less at peace with themselves, much more so than others.

The second point affecting much of the black race in America revealing the presence of the consequences of the fetish tree in their lives is:

Violence: This serves as proof of the effects of occult rituals in Afro-Americans' lives. The violence that is rampant in the black community. The killings, the rapes, and the drugs all could be the result of the transformation into the animal state that slaves went through after their passage by the fetish tree. Remember, one of the roles of that tree was to turn the slave into an animal. This can define the violent character which defines the African American. A minority of black folks are kind, determined to succeed in life, and at peace; others prefer living in their violent state. They are quick to react with violence. They are fit for all kinds of betrayal, ready to shoot each other in cold blooded murders; as it is regularly observed in predominantly black areas, and in some American streets.

Capable young African Americans drop out of school, to invest their energy in criminal activities. This results in frustration and drugs which gives way to violence and creates an unhealthy environment.

According to Article I, Section 2, of the United States Constitution of 1787, it states: *"For the purposes of representation in Congress, blacks enslaved in a state would be counted as three-fifths of the number of white inhabitants of this state."*

In my opinion, it is easy to understand that they had come to this American land to be used as separate beings. Who for others were comparable to the beast, to be exploited for the field and have no rights. It would not be surprising if, at that time, the whip was the means to execute and to make the black slave obey. This is all a shock every time I think about it.

Africa was virgin and wild when slave traders arrived. Our forefathers had to be heartless and ruthless to sell their brothers to strangers for worthless things. More so, for rending them defenseless to the point that whipping them was the way to make them understand what was expected of them. Thus, white Americans writing in the constitution that black people were not 100 percent human, was by no means to be faulted. That is what we black folks asked for; that's the way our ancestors wanted them to treat our race. Now, we see the animosity, the fractions, the hatred, and the killings of black Americans among themselves. We see how heartless they are towards people of the same skin color. Isn't that a curse? Going around the fetish tree for the last time implanted in them the star of submission which the Europeans saw and exploited without hesitation.

That last turn around the tree caused them to lead an angry life and that has been passed down from generation to generation.

Most of Dr. Martin Luther King Jr.'s messages were based on peace. He encouraged African Americans to respond to the abuse they faced with nonviolence. Dr. King certainly understood that the only way to deliver his brothers was to get them to abandon violent methods. That is why he prescribed love even for those who created segregation. His messages were real solutions, in my opinion; for in order to defeat the devil, one must give him love. Nonviolence would bring black folks into a fluid and positive spirit, giving them more understanding about the life they have been leading since the end of slavery.

The Bible makes it clear that those who live in an animal state will not be able to receive divine guidance necessary for a successful life; but only the one who lives in spirit can receive the father's secrets. (1 Corinthians 2:10-14). To live in spirit is to be filled with light; and only those who cultivate love, say no to violence, and living like animals can achieve that. If African Americans keep using violence, it will not benefit them in any way. That is Dr. King's message, to bring his brothers back to the light, to reverse the spell cast by ancestors from Africa. But above all, to annihilate the oppressions initiated by white people who wanted to see them drown in negativity.

He was probably murdered by those who understood his rescue strategy, and knew that with his momentum, African Americans were on their way to take over. How else can we explain the murder of a man who preached messages of peace, love, and nonviolence in a country where racial segregation prevailed? How can one understand the murder of a man who called his people, who were victims of injustice and inhuman treatment, to respond with love? Martin Luther King Jr. was well on his way to ending the violence and frustration for my cousins. He was a real blessing and hope for a better future. Unfortunately, the much-desired change never happened. The violence remains.

It is important to pause after these two extremely sensitive points for a conscience analysis. If you are my cousin, reading this book, and recognize these two points in your life, the following statement will allow you begin operation **X** by rejecting this evil out of your life.

"Today, I reject violence. Today, my eyes are open to apart of my life and I, (insert your name), chose a better life than the one I lead. I refuse and completely reject violence. I call on my true identity and to who I am supposed to be. I stand by my words and declare that I am a complete person and chosen by God. I am God's will on earth, I am God's peace established in my body, mind, and soul. I am now filled with the divine light, divine spirit, and my identity has been totally revealed to me. I am what God chose me to be, I am God's will on earth."

This statement must be repeated several times consciously at least three times a day, over a period of twenty-one days, to reprogram the subconscious by feeding it new information. There are similar audio statements on YouTube that you can listen to regularly to change your life. I can suggest a few that you can try.

Here is a prayer by St. Francis of Assisi, which I also recommend. It is very sensitive and effective. I have personally experienced it.

Lord,

Make me an instrument of your peace.

Where there is hatred, let me sow love.

Where there is injury, pardon.

Where there is doubt, faith.

Where there is despair, hope.

Where there is darkness, light.

Where there is sadness, joy.

O, Divine Master,

Grant that I may not so much seek.

To be consoled as to console.

To be understood as to understand.

To be loved as to love.

For it is in giving that we receive.

It is in pardoning that we are pardoned.

It is in dying that we are born to eternal life.

-St. Francis of Assisi

The last two points causing the horrible curse from which my cousins are suffering are:

Personality Confusion: Two young ladies once had a very touching conversation in my presence. One of them complained about her fiancé, whom she had just separated from for the simple reason that he was not responsible. They lived together in an apartment they rented for eight hundred dollars, but the fiancé in question was unable to pay the rent. Ironically, he committed to buying a brand-new Bentley for nearly sixty thousand dollars. The question that comes to mind here is: what kind of man is he? Most African American men tend to show off like they need to prove that they are important, whether they are poorly dressed or not. They want to be respected, to be put on a pedestal they never deserved to be on. They want to be considered free men able to do as they please, like it's important that others know they are not slaves anymore. They want to be seen as important and they seek all this in material or flashy things, and often times, in an insulting language; not realizing that they are doing the opposite of what they expect from others.

One important thing the slaves left in the fetish tree or in the river of the last bath is personality. After that was taken from the depths of their subconscious, nothing was left in them but pride and selfishness. My cousins are now trying to affirm a personality that is absent. They think they can find it in the vein things they accumulate, which rather show their poor traits of character.

The young fiancé who committed to buying a sixty thousand dollars car without being able to pay his eight hundred dollars rent, only thought of how relatives will view him driving such a car. He didn't care much about securing a roof over his head. The most important thing to him was the value or importance that would be attributed to him driving a Bentley. Obviously, he was looking for what he might never have had; he desired a place his forefathers never reserved for him. The black occult power applied against black folks results in a huge loss for everyone. Not only have they been sold, but they have also been stripped of the very essence which would have helped them to better understand life and make wise decisions in their lives.

Perdition: I stated earlier that black slaves were executing their tasks by the master's whip. This was not because they were not intelligent, but simply because they didn't understand the language spoken to them. A language is linked to a certain culture. The tree of oblivion took their culture from them; the last river bath kept their culture. One's culture defines one's notion of savoir vivre and bring one back to one's upbringing. If the slaves forgot where they came from, then they automatically forgot their culture. Culture would have allowed my cousins to trace their origin and regain their identity. They were sent to be lost. I understand that the provisions of the fetish tree, and the last bath river established by our ancestors, were such that the children who were sold as slaves were to never be heard of again. So, everything was done to make sure the slaves would never be seen again. Once the slaves left, they never were to be able to retrace their steps; they were to be lost forever and not remember where they came from.

The deeper you go, the more uncomfortable it gets. No one knows how deeply affected I am by the facts I am revealing in this book. It is immoral to decide to send one's brother to be lost. It is criminal to agree with the fact that one's brother goes away for a life of suffering, never to return. My African American cousins are lost in every possible way. They are physically and spiritually lost; they are morally and mentally lost; they're lost and are doomed to never be put back together.

In a word, the fetish tree and the river of the last bath are symbols of reinforcement for the curse of slavery. The fetish tree, particularly, embodied the spiritual prison for the souls of the slaves. It was an instrument of misfortune for them since its inception and is still in effect in the lives of their descendants. I am rather delighted to be able to bring out all these painful aspects of the African Americans everyday life, in order to help them in my own way to better understand their situation, and deal with it.

"I am present in spirit. I have a direction for my life. I believe and I affirm that my personality is regained. I have found my ancestors' lost path, and I trace it back to the source to build a better and dignified life from now on. I can now figure out who I am. I control all desires that contribute nothing to my life, and I reject them now to give way to a better life. I am who the Divine wants me to be. I am the salt of the earth. I am the light of the world. I am a city built on a hill. (Mathew 5: 13-14). I am full of flavor, and I will never be trampled or rejected again."

This is a second statement that can be repeated as the previous one to reprogram the subconscious. More solution proposals are coming in the upcoming chapters.

CHAPTER V

DIGNITY OR NON-DIGNITY

I would like to talk about a situation that shocked the Los Angeles African American community on Sunday, March 31, 2019. The rapper, Nipsey Hussle, 33, was murdered by a young black man. I feel helpless and would like to pay tribute to a man who, at some point in his life, understood that it was necessary to do something to help his community thrive. If, like me, you agree that this huge loss is an irreparable damage, then you will approve of this overly sensitive chapter on dignity in which I challenge all of us blacks, whether Africans or African Americans.

The behavior we see in black people stems from the absence of personality. One cannot speak of dignity without the individual's core values according to his origin. Dignity varies from one country to another; one ethnicity to another; one religion to another; one culture to another. But where do they come from? To what ethnic group do my cousins belong? These questions cannot be answered today, and in this case, the question of dignity will simply be set aside.

Dignity or non-dignity, a thorough analysis of the Afro-Americans' behaviors is needed. I have been watching my cousins carefully for at least ten years. I took my time to make comparisons. I have had the opportunity to be in direct contact with some, even for short periods of time. I talked to some to study the way they think. I still to this day wonder who they are. They are always looking for a vain glory, for the importance they would like others to give them, for a place that is not theirs, and are willing to do anything to be there. They are ready to betray each other, to kill themselves, and above all, to participate in the various low blows to get there. Their thinking is often superficial; they never take the time to make calculations, and especially to think about the consequences of their actions. I am not judging my cousins, I am just saying that most black folks, whether Africans, African Americans or otherwise, are sometimes similar when it comes to making certain decisions impacting their lives.

An example is our ancestors' decision to sell their own flesh and blood. I am convinced that our forefathers did not think about the consequences of the actions they were going to take. They just thought about their immediate profit and about how important they were going to be in their village. Black folks sometimes act without reason, and this is still going on today, whether in Africa or elsewhere.

The hardships my black cousins go through day in, and day out, hurts. Knowing that other racial groups see them as nobodies is heartbreaking. The black race is looked down upon by a world which gives it no consideration. What is even more disheartening is that there is no solution in sight to bring the slightest dignity to this race. We must look for the link that keeps this race in the molds of curse and manipulation. There is no dignity, and my heart still bleeds because I don't know if it will ever reappear.

My soul cries out for the fact that dignity has been sold at the price of junk. Dignity has been lost by innocence and ignorance, by the prediction of the future with the absence of awareness.

By talking about the absence of personality, I am simply referring to the occult practices that have been implemented to facilitate this trade. Our ancestors facilitated the purchase of their brothers by the white traders, and that brought about consequences; consequences still affecting millions of individuals today. All the challenges faced by black folks: violence, rape, killings, drugs, filth, etc. stem from not knowing who they are. They would know if only they had a personality in them which dictated to them what their human side should be. Their animal side often takes the lead, and that side cares nothing about dignity; and we must understand that all this, as I have been saying since the start, is spiritual.

An individual's personality reflects what the individual's consciousness dictates to him; and that consciousness often depends on the subconscious. So, if this subconscious has been altered to cause the individual to lose most of his faculties, then the personality will be devoid of certain data. Especially since the consciousness receives nothing from the subconscious. For someone to be violent, they were violent from their life's spiritual source. For them to be a killer, they were a killer from the source. To be morally unfit, they had to be unfit from the source. When we see an individual with no moral values, it started at the spiritual source. To heal this person, one must cleanse the spiritual bases to wipe out the negative elements operating there.

Dignity means that the conscience is mature about respecting the human being and is formed at an early age. We can talk about dignity when basic education has been imparted to guide the conscience into the future. That is, if the subconscious received data from birth that could guide the individual's personality into adulthood. It is no surprise really that this is nonexistent in my Afro-American cousins.

The basic upbringing we just talked about hasn't existed in the African American culture since the beginning. The slaves came to this country to live in bondage; and he who lives in bondage must necessarily have a master, and the master always decides what to do with him. Black folks still suffer from several curses which originated from several sources other than the occult practices I denounce in this book.

According to history, slaves were sold, and resold from one master to another. They were sold as cattle were sold on a farm. Nothing could prevent a master to sell his slave to another when he wanted at the price he decided. The worst and shocking thing about all this is when the slave woman gave birth, she only had time to breastfeed her child, see him grow a bit, then the master could make money by selling that child. The issue with that picture is that this particular child inherited no knowledge except for bondage; and above all will grow up without a proper upbringing, and without knowing anything of his origin. No one gave him dignity or respect. The child's subconscious didn't register any information that his conscience could use when came the time to form his personality. So, the slave's child who was sold at a young age not only grew up, but also opened his eyes in bondage, in slavery. He ended up becoming a man without moral values and dignity. This child's case did not end there; the lack of proper upbringing, and respect was passed down from generation to generation. The bondage and animal status were transmitted from generation to generation because that was all that subconscious knew.

Now let us look back to visualize the mother who was deprived of her child. The mother who saw her son or daughter being sold. Feel her pain if you can; imagine it a little. Picture the aftermath of her child being taken away from her. That left a mark in her forever which could never be erased. This leads to the conclusion that all my cousins were to their masters really, were dressed up animals.

No wonder white folks considered them less than humans. What legacy of dignity could have been left to black women during those times, if not only the act of breastfeeding and caring for their children a little while. The same picture is what we see today. Afro-American mothers taking care of their child from birth until teenage years with absent fathers. Then, the child is left to fend for himself most of the time, which I define as selling one's child to nature. Inevitably, the child grows up without personality. None of what we observe today in the black community is new. It is just the continuity of old patterns, and it is not about to stop. A curse which complements that of the tree.

The Afro-American fathers' situation is not much different from that of the mothers' aforementioned. Let's demonstrate why black American men get girls pregnant, and never take responsibility for any of the children they father.

One day, very early in the morning, I picked up a young black man in southwest Washington, D.C. He was in a state of distress. When I asked him what was wrong, I was surprised by his answer. He had been out of a job for over three months and was going out that morning to try his luck. He continued, saying he had seven children with seven different women, and was to pay child support to each one of them every month. The women had taken him to court to force him to take responsibility for his children.

I did not expect the response he gave me at all; seven children from seven women? That was a shocker! That young man, who was about my age, would have to work all his life to help the women take care of his children, or else he was headed to prison. If this young man were in a normal state, if his conscience dictated a certain morality to his being, he would not have found himself in such a situation.

Back in the day, the slave was allowed to have pleasure by his master. He only slept with a woman with his master's permission, and if the woman were to become pregnant, the slave was not responsible. The master had power over the child and could sell him whenever he felt like it. We cannot ask the Afro-American man to be responsible; we can't ask him to be a dad. He's only a parent, because he got a lady pregnant, and had a child. Every man can be a father; but it takes a lot more than bringing a child into the world to be a dad. A dad takes on all the different responsibilities towards his children.

Most of my Afro-American cousins are just parents because they do not care for their children. Black people did not live as a family, perhaps as a community they did, but not as a family. The female slave did not actually have a husband, nor did the man have a wife. They all lived with their master who supervised and fed them like cattle were fed. So, a normal family setting hardly existed, and they can't be blamed for that. At the source, information is needed to be used for the personality formation.

The lack of dignity in my cousins is spiritual. Since the creation of the world, and since I was born, I have not yet heard that a tree gives the fruit of another tree. It's all in the root. The root is the origin, and from it stems everything that is necessary in our lives. One does not live in assumption and must have a source to question sometimes. My American cousins, successful or not, don't have that unless they underwent a spiritual transformation. I am sorry I point in this direction, but since it is important to take this path to demonstrate the reality my cousins are living, I am forced to talk about it to offer a clear understanding to the world which otherwise judge them.

Dignity sleeps in my cousins because there is nothing to awaken and nourish it. Dignity is silent because there is nothing to water it and help it flourish. Dignity is dying because it needs the educational oxygen from the positive sources of the being that they are. Dignity no longer lives in them because many other things took its place. This translates into a huge loss for the world.

My aim is also to let us all know that no one has been created to be in such a state, to live what the African Americans are going through today. Perdition in full swing! Every day black children are being born for the continuation of this unacceptable evil. The lack of personality which takes away dignity and respect so desired by their forefathers will live on with the new, innocent generation.

Another aspect of the situation I would like to address is the fact that most girls in the black community today are pregnant at fourteen or sixteen-years-old, just like their mothers. And like their mothers, they don't attend college simply because the girls watch their mothers do what their grandmothers did. At thirty, they are grandmothers, and at forty-five they are great-grandmothers. Just because that's what the invisible system knows and transmits to them.

My American cousins would have loved to replace the master today; to be respected in the eyes of their community. But to no avail do they entertain their wishful thinking; none of it comes to pass because it was not established from the start.

Their way of feeding their ego is by wearing big shoes, big pants, big and long chains around the neck, their demeanor, their way of speaking. They seek a nonexistent dignity. My cousins acknowledge something absent in them; and it is their invisible value that is to give them back respect and human trait.

Afro-American men, holding fifty-dollar bills and counting them in the eyes of all; just to show his entourage that he is rich. Ladies, with very large, long artificial nails and eyelashes; young boys with their pants down to the buttocks with a staggering demeanor, arms raised like an eagle preparing to fly, and so on.

The absent value, yet so sought, is the reason for all this. Understand from this moment on, my cousins playing music in the car so loud it disturbs others; it's just that everyone has to notice them in a car that may not be theirs, for them to feel important in the moment. Please understand the girl who shows up with several hair colors with extravagant lipstick. I am explaining all this to get everyone to understand what the problem is and, above all, offer a solution. I am saying this so that we stop marginalizing my cousins; stop judging them and treating them as less than nothing. We need to start by understanding them and helping them out of their spiritual prison.

We need worthy people to help others find their true path in life. I am talking about dignity because it is a sensitive parameter of a moral and better life. A community which doesn't have it will find it challenging to evolve.

One day, I met a white woman who was going to a church in Southeast Washington, D.C. She was to give psychotherapy sessions to prisoners who were released and were struggling to reintegrate society. This lady said, *"I understand them as well as what is happening to them, which is why it is easy for me to approach and talk to them."* She went on to say, *"They didn't get there because they want to, but just because they don't know how to go about things. They don't know how to do things. Black people are in jail because they smoke drugs wherever they want. White people know that they better do their drugs in the bedroom."* I get what she meant by black folks smoke their drugs outside.

They lack some knowledge about the jungle they live in. The lady touched on an important aspect of black peoples' lives when she mentioned that they did not get to where they are today because they want to. The system in which they opened their eyes does not recognize them and they still do not master it. When I talk about the system, I mean their freedom. The type of freedom that was given to black Americans was just a system they were put into to keep them from evolving. They do not yet understand the meaning of their freedom. They still don't know how that freedom of theirs should be managed. In the past, the slave was fed under his master's authority; today, he is free without resources and without reference.

African Americans want the good life without knowing what it takes to have it. They want prosperity without knowing the path to prosperity. They want happiness, but they are extremely far from that happiness. Their soul has been emptied from Africa. Their subconscious has no reference that can help them. To have some dignity, you need to have been raised by someone of good character. The black folks' lost dignity, which origin we have discovered, has its source in what I call, 'the pride's absence from the soul.' The selfish pride of the blood which delivered his own for junk. The pride of wickedness which erased the traces of his brother by selling him without remorse to own vain possessions. One must understand, try to find the truth which reveals the good side of my cousins and the reality they face daily.

Who killed Malcolm X? A young black man. No one can explain why he committed that crime. But, in my opinion, the will to kill the human rights activist did not come from him. I don't know how the status of Malcolm X, hindered this twenty-four-year-old man. I do not know how Malcolm X's struggle bothered Thomas Hagan. I don't see how his advocacy and teachings constituted a problem to the young man he was. What drove him to commit such an evil act if not the lack of dignity in him that was used by those around him who resented Malcolm X. They brainwashed him, played tricks on his mind, promising him that he could become important and respected in the eyes of his community. A glory that led him straight to prison; prison that the twenty-four-year-old man didn't even think of when his head was being filled up. So, he agreed to lend his body to the devil for a precarious celebrity.

The slave has no conscience, no respect for his own person; that has been established since the beginning of slavery. The slave is easily convinced and manipulated because he is naïve. It is this same naivete that the northern states of the United States of America understood by fighting in 1866 for the civil rights of newly freed slaves; whom they used to have the majority of the seats in the Senate. This sparked the creation of the Ku Klux Klan in the southern states to kill slaves and burn them alive so that the rights they had just obtained, would not benefit them. The slave always lost and paid the price for white folks' cunning against them. There is no dignity or personality in the daily lives of ghetto Afro-Americans; because they were not raised under the conditions required for that dignity. They were raised worthless, to be worthless.

Someone told me that they are cursed, and it was a shock to hear that. However, I held back from reacting. I internalized my anger for days. That statement ate at me for quite a while. I analyzed it for days to understand the basis for him saying that African Americans are cursed. My conclusion is that he expressed in his own way what he witnesses daily in my cousins' lives, and concluded that to live such a life, one must be cursed. Prisons are full of black people, not because they made that choice, but rather because they were already oriented to these prisons from birth.

Dignity is absent for the simple reason that basic upbringing is nonexistent. Upbringing is an important reference regardless of your origin, and this is based on very strict rules and principles to observe to be a respectable human being. But who is the guarantor of this educational support for my cousins? They are referred from an early age to a school which does not give them any guarantee about their future. The truth is that the educational system, whether at home or school, must be able to lead to the development of a personality; from that comes dignity. If there is no minimum upbringing educational support neither at home, nor at school or the streets, and television take over, then of course problems can be expected in the future. The father, who is supposed to be the most important figure in the upbringing of his children, is either absent or has no knowledge in the matter. In that case, where does the child find his dignity?

Dignity is often family-based; it is a family inheritance transmitted from one generation to another. With the notion of family being absent among Afro-Americans, dignity is also automatically absent. The notion of family and dignity is violated within the black American race, with everyone doing what they please, whenever they want.

Dignity or no dignity? The answer is no dignity; and this hurts because it proves the extent to which everything has been taken away from the slaves. They were ripped of everything and left without resource. Dignity or no dignity? I believe that they came to the United States of America and left their homeland with no dignity, because they no longer knew of their tradition; all that they would have received from their parents. Black folks live because they were given life. They live to exist and walk a dark path with no way out, under a status of freedom that bears no positive results. Dignity or no dignity? They were betrayed by their own brethren and remained in the vision of not recognizing each other because they had a master who ordered them around. My African American cousins are suffering. They have accepted their fate, continue living as if things were normal, and this suffering is sinking them. The best way to live is to accept what one is going through and make one's home a paradise. They have accepted their difficult fate without considering the rest in their life.

CHAPTER VI

THE SPIRITUAL CHARACTER OF SLAVERY

The visualization of reality in the spiritual world is quite different than in the physical world. History has left scars on black folks' lives. History has made it possible to build museums and trace the misfortune slaves went through throughout three centuries. Considering the fact that we recognize the story in its physicality; it is important to go further so as to bring out the spiritual traces that history decided to set aside. I am interested in understanding slavery in its spiritual sense, and to know whether slavery is a curse in its own spiritual aspect.

My analysis in this sixth chapter is based on references in the holy book, 'The Bible'. In the book of Genesis, history tells us about Joseph, a Jew who became a great ruler in Egypt. According to the Bible, Joseph didn't go to Egypt in quest of an adventure or business; he was sold by his own brothers to a stranger. Even though he came from a line of noble men, his bloodline of a dignified son of Jacob was converted into that of a slave, which brought a curse on the young Joseph. When we look for the origin of this curse, we discover the stages by which Joseph took; namely prison, the house of Putiphar where he was master before returning to prison, then moved to the palace of the pharaoh, and finally when he died, he was buried among his people.

Joseph did not receive any tribute from pharaoh or from any of his ministers. After his death, he was simply buried among his own. The fate of this son of Israel, ancestor of the Israelite descendants in Egypt, fell upon all his people after his death, and they all were made slaves. The curse of their ancestors who had arrived in Egypt in chains took place, because things had to run their course according to plans for a well-defined reason.

I only brought Joseph's example up to demonstrate something: slavery is pure curse; we must recognize and accept it. This also helps us understand things these days through my cousins' lives in the United States of America.

If Joseph would have gone to Egypt any other way, his people would not have been struck by the evil of servitude. As a result, the slave curse, still active, has them fighting for a place to call home. The territorial war, going on for years between the Israelis and the Palestinians, is proof that Joseph's curse is still at work although his people has been chosen by the supreme God Himself. I am not trying to judge, insult, or call the people of Israel miserable; I greatly admire them, and they are a source of a spiritual inspiration to me. I am just trying to understand the reason for their conversion from free to slaves through their experience in Egypt. I want to understand their reaction after their liberation and compare it to that of African Americans.

Let's now review the life of Moses, who was born to Israeli and slave parents; but was raised in the luxury of pharaoh's palace. Whom dressed and was educated as an Egyptian. This Hebrew, who only knew the Egyptian culture and gods, also ended up with his slave people before fulfilling his mission as a liberator. So, looking at these two men's (Joseph and Moses) lives, we cannot help but draw the conclusion that slavery is a curse that prevails over several generations, supported by the blood flowing in the veins of the slaves' offspring.

I mention the blood because this vital liquid is spiritual, powerful, and adds value to your life according to your origin. Blood has a strong spiritual bond with the soul, for the soul is in the blood, and blood is the soul. It is the summary of the sources from which one comes. One's life is defined according to what flows through one's veins; and on that basis, one's evolution is established. That is why we talk about royal blood, the blood of the poor, the blood of the slaves, the blood of the rich.

So, the second powerful aspect of slavery is in the blood. It is to be noted that slave blood is not a royal blood, which means that it is difficult for a slave to be king. It also means that it is not likely for an African American, whose ancestors came to this country in chains and sold as a slave, to become President of the United States. Unless there has been a correction through a fusion with royal blood. We must understand today that the election of Barack OBAMA is not yet the fulfillment of Martin Luther King Jr.'s dream. A descendant of a slave has not yet been elected president of this country.

My cousins still have a long way to go for Martin Luther King Jr.'s dream to be fulfilled. I will explain more. Barack OBAMA is not a slave; genetically, he is a black man, but not a descendant of slaves. His father did not come to the United States sold and in chains. He came here as a student, which makes a huge difference. Moreover, Obama's mother was not black. She was a white woman. If the OBAMA family tree was explored, there could be royalty in his paternal family over three or even several generations ago. The blood that runs through Obama's veins, is not of slave blood.

Spiritual lineage doesn't allow for the grandiose election this man had to the White House; only royal blood does. So, there is a difference between someone who was chosen king, and one who usurped the king's throne. They both manage very differently; their instinct totally differs; their skill is different; and their understanding of royalty is definitely different. When a person truly in a royal covenant is elected king, or president, the citizens are happy during his tenure. But when it is the other way around, people suffer because the illegal ruler has no idea who he is, plus the throne was never intended for him.

So, Obama, by his blood, was president because he is not a descendant of a slave. His wife, Michelle, may be from a slave lineage, but there is something called: spiritual justification and transfiguration through the bonds of marriage. The sacred bonds of marriage cleansed Michelle of the slave curse; especially if the blood flowing in her husband's veins is spiritually strong blood and is of a royal origin; or the man is from a wealthy family.

In the story about Merlin of the Kingdom of Camelot, the servant, Guinevere, became Queen after the death of King Arthur, her husband. He fell under the spell of his sister, Morgan's, maid. She became Prince Arthur's wife the day after the death of King Uther Pendragon. She was thus justified and made fit for the rank of Queen by the sacred bonds of marriage.

Her blood as a servant underwent a change by the marriage bond which allowed Guinevere to become Queen. As a slave descendant, Michelle Obama was in the white house; but before then, she had been totally freed from the curse of slavery; or at least justified by the marriage bond. Also, she is just half descendant of slave and not one hundred percent so.

It is important to know blood can bring good or evil upon us spiritually. Michelle Obama could have been a source of misfortune for Barack, and vice versa. A female with slave blood can bring unhappiness to her husband who is not of slave origin. A man descended from a slave by the marriage bond can bring misfortune to his wife, because of the blood flowing in him. Not only slaves are a cause of misfortune though; I just keep the focus on them, because this book is about them.

It is important then to understand that some Afro-Americans, who are elected governors, mayors, or who hold an important office, very often, and in general, come from mixed sources. They are not one hundred percent descendants of slaves. Most of the mixing originated from the masters sleeping with their slave maids and getting them pregnant. Those children's paternity was never established, but that later gave their descendants the chance to partially eliminate the curses.

The third spiritual aspect that I would like to highlight, is a very profound spiritual act that has intensified the slavery curse. When the slave gave birth, the child was snatched from her at a certain age and sold. The same way a slave was sold from one master to another if he was not docile. Let us try to understand what could have happened with the children who were sold. They were likely to end up loving each other and getting married. Brothers and sisters marry each other without knowing that they came from the same womb. The descendants from the couple carry the same blood and were a product of incest recognized by spiritual laws, and to whom the invisible sentences of incest were applied as well as to future generations. This sort of thing can accentuate the curse emerging from the life of bondage in the sense that any descendant of the incestuous couple run the risk of a stronger curse than the normal descendants we talked about. The curse was reinforced by the same blood intensity from their common parent.

Slavery in its spiritual color touches several aspects and doesn't allow the slaves' descendants to live a successful life. The very deep wounds the inhumane slavery trade left, will always remain; their spiritual character does not offer the slaves' offspring a way out. The descendants' life often has a bitter taste to it; life doesn't give them much but disguised servitude. Being a descendant of a slave is not a crime; one just faces the challenge of how to orient one's life, especially being able to choose the right partner. One must be aware of the blood that flows in one's veins, and work for a transfiguration. No one chose to be a slave's descendant, but if that is the case, then one needs to tirelessly do spiritual work in order to change one's mental programming.

I am disheartened for these generations who can't explain what is happening to them, and why they face the challenges they are confronted with. I am sad because they have no knowledge about the life they lead, and no choice but to live it.

EQUAL BUT SEPARATE - JIM CROW LAWS:

The Jim Crow Laws; I would like to explore these laws in its spiritual sense. The Jim Crow laws came to be after slavery ended. This defined the separation on several points between blacks and whites. Those who established these laws did not do so just for segregation purposes, but mainly for spiritual reasons. It was out of the question to let the savages' blood get mixed up with theirs. It was not conceivable that yesteryear's animals could now sit at the same table as the masters; drink at the same fountain, eat from the same plates at a restaurant. In essence, these laws were primarily spiritual, and intended to prevent prosperity from being tainted by the black race's misfortune. Those who drafted the Jim Crow laws were not mere doctors of the law, but also people belonging to brotherhoods, sects, and various fraternities. These people mastered spiritual skills, especially concerning prosperity. It was, therefore, necessary to define the parameters of the laws in such a way that black folks were not admitted in the same circles as whites. They didn't want to take the chance of running into misfortune. The blacks were in fact considered the crown of curse and could spread it. After the abolition of slavery, the greatest precaution to take was to put safeguards in place so that the negative egregor of the liberated did not get mixed up with the fields of prosperity created by the masters.

Jim Crow laws appeared in the southern states, which did not want to mix slaves with their heritage. Thus, blacks were forbidden to visit the same public places as their former masters; restaurants, public transport, and more were separated. A black man could not marry a white woman. All this came from a spiritual reflection, according to which a mixture of energies should be avoided. The energy from the blacks was automatically perceived as negative. Anyone who accepted the marriage of his child to a black person could jeopardize his family's stability. The segregation in its spiritual sense, was to reject all that came from black folks, at that point in time. The white folks feared their future generations would be relegated to the former slaves' position. They were scared that the animals would occupy a high position in society when their blood would have been corrected by a possible marriage bond. They feared the naturally intelligent and brave slaves would receive the same school education as their children and might one day go beyond their expectations. They feared being ruled by a slave one day.

Jim Crow laws was to prevent a spiritual mixture of the slave blood, to that of the master's; and deny the fusion of their energies. At that time, the black person's energy was generally one of submission, fear, and bondage. That energy could not build a nation. So, by agreeing to merge and share with the former slaves, they might one day have become like them. Segregation has not completely disappeared today. It is difficult for some white families to see their child as a descendant of the black race.

In conclusion, my cousins must work to cleanse their aura of the negativity that clings to them, and which often creates a repulsion on the part of those who do not know them. Especially white people who are gradually getting used to their ways.

Slavery is a curse whether we accept it or not. Anyone who descended from this evil lineage must know that they must work to break several chains of curses.

CHAPTER VII

THE SO-CALLED SUCCESSFUL AFRICAN AMERICANS

I can't help but raise the issue of the few successful African Americans. It is true that some have had the opportunity to experience some level of happiness. Let me put it this way because this that has yet to be reviewed; the success of these black people can be explained in two respects:

First, it can be understood by the fact that not all slaves passed through the tree of oblivion, the last bath lake, etc. These means of spiritual transformation were implemented mainly in West Africa (Benin, Ghana, Côte d'Ivoire, etc.) after a long and violent resistance from the first slaves who fiercely opposed their forced expedition. It was, therefore, necessary to find a solution to master them. Hence, the fetish tree, the last bath, etc. (The few spiritual arrangements I have mentioned in previous chapters). Not all slaves were subjected to rituals at the beginning of the trade. It cannot be said with certainty that all slaves went through rituals of perdition; the same arrangements were not taken by the other countries that had engaged in this trade. Each country had its own way of preparing its slaves. It is understandable that some slaves, the very first for example, who left Benin and the surrounding areas, did not pass through this tree. Therefore, they came with all their senses and even part of their culture. This explains the presence of the Vodou cult in Brazil, the West Indies, Haiti, and even in the state of Louisiana in the United States of America, today. This has somehow limited the curses, while retaining the slave blood still crying out in their lives. Spiritual corrections can be made unconsciously while keeping the slave aspect of them. That is why their success is often limited even though they are wealthy. A slave cannot be the master while the latter still is. The emphasis will, therefore, be put on their limitation in success and sometimes the unhappy end of their lives.

The second aspect that can justify this success is the mixing; the interracial relationships between slaves and masters. African beauty is of an irresistible quality which were noticed by some white men. Some slaves were raped by their masters and sometimes impregnated. Frederick Douglas, the emblematic figure of the Black American race, is living proof of relationships between a master and his slave. As a child, Douglas was never recognized by his white father and was considered a slave. Which means that even though his blood was mixed, he still had the slave stain on him.

Frederick Douglas grew up as a slave, but his future would be totally different from a child born as one hundred percent slave. This justifies the fact that some of these successful Afro-Americans are actually mostly mulattos. They retain their mothers' black heritage symbol of the rejection by their white biological father.

Another situation that might also benefit slaves' descendants, which I would only like to mention briefly, is the commitment of some so-called successful ones to sects, esoteric societies, or fraternities. This though, I will not talk about so as not to make gratuitous assertions. This subject requires further research to prove what I am writing.

With regards to the very notion of success, talking about the so-called successful black cousins, I am sometimes puzzled, and think it is just the false appearance of success. The real question is whether they really had the life, identity, or even the happiness they desired in this success.

History does not mention black people who came up with scientific inventions. The system put in place by the former master is not eager to praise the former slaves who made contributions to the success of the United States of America and certain countries in the world. By doing so, it gives no hope to the younger black generations. In reality, the United States of America, according to the system, belongs to the white race who must be served by black folks.

I see things differently today with regards to the so-called successful black people, because in my humble opinion, success must normally benefit the community to which we belong.

Black folks though, whether in the United States of America, Africa, or elsewhere, have a long-standing problem: self-centeredness which makes us want to keep fame to ourselves. This is one of the reasons that explains us selling our own brothers to the white slave traders. Many people might not agree with me on this point, but it must be said; if only to awake the conscience of African American youth, a youth with an uncertain future.

In fact, the so-called successful black people are very few. And of these, most did not fully experience the life they wanted because the lack of personality was not in their favor. Great American football players, famous basketball players, journalists, singers, actors, filmmakers; majority of black folks ended up losing the fortune they made.

Consider for example, the famous Michael Jackson. He was born with a tremendous talent which guaranteed a bright, successful, and prosperous future. Michael marveled the world at an early age. He was highly favored among his brothers, but he lacked something; Michael felt that something was missing in him. I can tell you for sure that it was his personality, his identity. Who was he really in this world? His subconscious shared nothing with him about what he lacked; there was a void that he could not explain. The absence of spiritual identification taught him nothing about the reason for his prosperity, his success, his wealth. Michael did not understand why he was at that level, because the blood flowing through his veins was slave blood, a blood stained with unknown curses.

He could not continue living in that internal void, heavy with unanswered questions. He had to regain his missing personality, identity, and personal divinity through his subconscious that had remained silent since his forefathers. So, he tried changing his skin color, his facial features, his hair, hoping that maybe the emptiness within him could be filled. Michael made lots of money, built all he wanted, created his own world. In a nutshell, he had everything he desired except for three things: his origin, his subconscious, and his personality. He never had an identity because there was no one to direct him to his source. He struggled with that throughout his life and brilliant singing career. All the changes he put his body through proves it and led him to drift. He always felt tied up in the invisible, because spiritually he lacked the identity and the personality that he needed for his life to be fulfilled as he wished; for him to fully enjoy it.

There is no denying the success of some black people. But the fact that our race is still referred to as the lowest class in the United States of America, refers to a deeper problem that finds its roots in the subconscious of our ancestors. It has been deprived of any information trapped in the fetish tree or wiped by other occult practices. This subconscious should have been able to provide guidance for the future. It was snatched away in Africa, and the slaves came to America practically empty. So, how many successful black Americans end their lives tragically or end up murdered?

If my cousins' success were stainless, the United States would already have been taken over by them, since their blood was shed to build this country. If their success had an impact in this country, many of them would no longer be in the ghettos. The success of my successful cousins is not yet beneficial to the black community because it is devoid of these spiritual rights.

However, black folks have some merits and must be respected by all others. We, the black race, are not lazy people. Nothing in this world has been built without the blood of the black race. It has been in the form of imprecation whether in Africa, Europe, America, or elsewhere in the world. Much of all the existing goods which benefit humanity comes from the goodness and gullibility of the black race.

The black race must exist and be what it is for the white race to be at their level in the world. Black is not as negative as seen or painted. The black color is of a great value that allows the other colors to shine. There won't be a white color without the black color; black must exist so that white can be perceived and appreciated as such.

In spite of the spiritual challenges, the black race has been a successful race since the beginning of time. It has been an abundantly rich race; one that has been long-established with a heart similar to that of a child. Which may be why others abuse it as they see fit.

Many of them succeed in this world, putting their intelligence into change and humanitarian solutions. There are many of them to whom we must pay great tribute for the valiant sacrifice of their lives.

The White House would not exist if black blood had not been shed to build it. Slaves' blood helped build that white masterpiece that the whole world comes to visit. France would not be the country it is today if black blood had not been shed in the world wars to defend it. Blacks' success is second to none and must be recognized at its fair value.

However, it is important to seriously acknowledge the profound aspect I reveal in this book. It is sensitive and paralyzes the momentum of our black brothers in the United States of America. This will be a great liberation for the whole world, and I will never be able to live without transmitting this message inspired by the divine spirit for my cousins there.

Any individual, whether black, white, yellow, or red; from any continent on this earth who once experienced slavery, or descends from a lineage that has experienced slavery, is already automatically in a complicated situation. This means that once one has been tainted with slavery, it is exceedingly difficult for future generations to establish themselves in their evolution. There have been several forms of slavery, and other races have experienced slavery in their own way. Starting with the example of the Jewish people who were once long enslaved in Egypt, and who were liberated according to the Bible, by the Supreme God, the Alpha and Omega. These people, whom the Bible calls *'the chosen of God'* over whom He poured his blessings, still have no peace. To this day, they must fight and wage wars to keep their country safe. To sum it up, descendants of a slavery lineage are often confronted with situations that have them fighting for a position in the world.

The people of Israel's example make me think even deeply about this subject. They were slaves in Egypt and still fight to position themselves in their environment. The Bible does not tell us about the recent captivity these Jewish endured after Jesus. Of the abuse they suffered, even more recently from Europeans, especially Germans. This means that long after slavery in Egypt, the domination of their own territory by the Romans and Jesus Christ, the Jewish experienced another form of slavery, captivity, and other forms of unhappiness, beside what the Bible mentioned. As a result, the continuing effect of slavery on a man's life is long-lasting. The spirit of bondage is so profound, that it never ceases to impact the lives of the concerned people. It takes a serious and constant fight to free oneself from such a sticky and ruthless spirit that can plague over thousands of years, passing on from generation to generation.

So, some of my cousins here may have succeeded, but their success could not have had a decisive impact on the black American community. The experience in countries where slaves have been resettled has been proven that they have not been able to do much with their new lives. They remained in a certain stagnation, and in many cases, continue to reach out to their former master.

In the United States of America, it is true that slaves have been freed, but it would be hard for them to experience real prosperity. Because not only have they been liberated on the land on which they were slaves, but they also continue living on that same land. That is not conducive to the success of the former slaves. That situation could not foster the necessary change in their lives because, despite their determination or their will to make a difference, the ever-present former masters would do anything to stifle them. It would indeed be difficult for the masters to realize or accept that their former servants took a different position. It would be difficult for the master to admit or imagine a reversal of the situation in which he the former master would find himself in a different position. You come across everyday situations, for example, in a restaurant, when a couple or a group of Afro-Americans want a white server to attend to them.

This kind of behavior is unacceptable. My wife and I often found ourselves in such instances even in high standing restaurants. One Valentine's Day, we went to dinner with friends in Washington, D.C. The manager had to discreetly change our white server because of her negative behavior towards us. It is very regrettable to still see such behaviors or feelings from the descendants of the former masters. These are attitudes that indicate that raising black folks to a certain social level will not be easy anytime soon, because they still live in the land of bondage.

In light of this, my black cousins living in the current conditions will find it difficult to achieve a success that could actually help future generations. That's why I titled this chapter, "THE SO-CALLED SUCCESSFUL BLACKS". There hasn't been any real change yet, no success story that can be recounted, as African Americans' efforts are smothered, and their achievements are undermined.

The observations made above clearly demonstrate that slavery is a true curse and that anyone who is part of a lineage which has experienced slavery needs a great determination in all his endeavors. And above all, a spiritual deliverance beforehand. Moreover, he would, as much as he can, need to move from the location his ancestors served as slaves. To support my previous remarks, I can say this: we often observe that Africans who arrived in the United States of America via an entry visa are more successful in their activities than slaves' descendants whose forefathers came to America in chains.

The most famous case is that of Barack OBAMA. He was never a slave. Yes, he is a Black man, but definitely not a descendant of an Obama slave. He probably was elected President of the United States because the blood flowing through his veins was never a slave blood. Neither his father, nor his mother was a slave. As noted above, we also observed that many of the successful black people are not fully slaves' descendants. It is, therefore, easy to understand that the spirit of bondage does not offer much opportunity of prosperity to slaves' descendants. Their actions are often suppressed. Black people who came up with many great inventions have always been kept hidden, ignored because the master was still not ready to accept that his slave might be smarter than him. The masters in question are still here; former masters' descendants as well as former slaves' descendants still live, carrying their inheritance and opinion about one another within.

As a result, the African American community must first accept the obvious. Then, must with special efforts, work to produce different results. A new position allowing them to perceive things differently and to approach in another way the reality that is theirs today; on a land where their ancestors were slaves.

The blood flowing in their veins remains that of slaves, which explains why what black people experience is the consequence of an original curse which continues to impact their lives.

My cousins need to find a way out of this frustration and face this bitter reality. Only they can decide whether to embrace change. That's when success will begin. Then a real strategy will be put in place to end any action to suffocate their works by former masters. Above all, there will now be a clearer understanding of all that needs to be done to ensure a better future for generations to come.

CHAPTER VIII

MORAL AND PHYSICAL RESOLUTION

In 2015 and 2016, a new wave of incidents occurred in the United States of America. Young black people were being cold bloodedly killed by white police officers. This led to the uprising of African Americans, which resulted in the destruction of property. Shops were looted and burned, police vehicles burned, and many other acts of vandalism were committed during these protests. We still remember the ones in the city of Baltimore, where a young man had died because the police had arrested him for some obscure reason. Baltimore, a city in northern Maryland, is one of the strongholds of Afro-Americans. For two days, the black community was heard both by the voice of its charismatic leaders, and by acts of violence to protest the killing of its members. Multiple heists, looting, and acts of violence will never be the appropriate answer to the injustice they face.

In response to the recent racist police killings, some wealthy African Americans made important decisions such as withdrawing their assets from banks considered to be white owned. By raising awareness, a real boycott movement was born against white businesses. The consumption of their products was another way for black folks to claim their respect and prove their importance. These actions, however vigorous, cannot, in my view, be a lasting solution to the unfortunate situation faced by this community.

African Americans' problem, as I described above, comes in two aspects: the physical moral aspect and the spiritual one. Therefore, any proposal for a solution to end their suffering in a lasting way, must also go both directions to address the real causes of the problem and truly break the misconceptions that marked the sad Ku Klux Klan era.

Breaking down the physical and moral chains that hold my Afro-American cousins in this country, must go through a firm resolution on their part. A total awareness that aims to bring order to their lives and that of their community. They need to incorporate the necessity for a real change in their thinking and this challenge is primarily one for the black American youth. Their parents certainly did not pass on to them historical, social values, and references. However, it is now up to them to take responsibility for themselves, to take responsibility for history by conquering these values. Not through violence, but through hard work, the development of strong community ties based on unity, and solidarity to defend their rights together and to be respected by others.

At this point, it is important to remember that black folks' freedom here is limited, even though they seem free to do what they want. The freedom in which remains captive and which I am talking about here is rather spiritual. The physical chains of slavery may have been removed, but the spiritual chains remain. Instead of keeping the focus on the spiritual note in this chapter, I will rather do so on the physical and moral aspect which is very important, and which can lead to spiritual resolution.

We have established that some of the many successful black people in the United States of America, have been able to escape the curse of the fetish tree, etc. However, I cannot stress enough the fact that even they could only partially escape the curse chain as will be further demonstrated in the next chapter. They are found in virtually every field: great international players, film actors, world-renowned singers, journalists, lawmen, police, etc. It is precisely up to them to play a fundamental role in the historic movement to reorganize things in their community.

Freedom is something you fight for. Courageous steps must be taken to conquer true and complete freedom. Freedom is only valued when you earn it by fighting for it. Those of my American cousins who, even though faced with the many blockages and curses, still managed to be financially well positioned and have earned the freedom fighter title. The change I envision in this book, precisely appeals to the rich black people from all walks of life, from every state of the United States of America. Nowadays, the success of such a work of change depends on financial means. A vision without money is a dead vision. It is, therefore, important to make resolutions aimed at unifying rich black folks to bring their energies together for the development of their community. It is important for them to create a synergy, a new dynamic that can profoundly change the current order and end their brothers suffering across the country.

All my successful cousins together can be a counterweight to the arbitrary, a solution, and great hope through their valuable contribution to solving the problems of the black community.

Building schools with appropriate educational programs, universities to facilitate access for many black children who cannot afford college tuition fees, awareness, and rehabilitation centers for people in trouble with the law. Modern hospitals, projects to produce basic necessities, shopping malls, and other development infrastructures can contribute to improving lives in the black communities. Those are initiatives for which I appeal to all my successful black brothers and sisters, all wealthy African Americans, through my book today.

This is the physical moral solution that I suggest creating some change that, even if not definitive, could open incredible doors for the appeasement of the suffering in black American communities. It involves breaking with the culture of individualism. This requires a real platform for change which is well thought through.

The outlook is favorable. Looking ahead to the future of today's black children, one feels bad because one still sees the same traps to which their parents were subjected without any reference. Fortunately, many of those young people today are willing to do what it takes to change their lives. They are willing to be responsible, create a family, and live happily with them. Leaving behind them the life of suffering for good. Only there is barely a way out, very little escape. Let us not forget, condemnation strikes from generation to generation with its procession of deviances.

In fact, when you approach African Americans, you realize that they are wonderful people and not as they are portrayed. It is true that many of their actions make one wonder, but frustrations are sometimes what lead them to wrongdoing. All over the world, there are good and bad people. The same is true of the black American community. To generalize prejudice would be to condemn this community to extinction without a cure.

We are stronger together, and the moral solution for the issues destroying this community requires its members to unite to change their image, to change the hereditary label. The question today is no longer who is the richest or the most famous of black folks, but rather how to save the dignity of the whole race by deeply reflecting on the unenviable fate that majority of my cousins share. It is time for concerted and effective actions to improve current conditions and project a better future for next generations.

This book makes suggestions to solve a worrying problem in which spiritual causes and solutions have long been ignored or despised. Its purpose is not to judge anyone. Its suggestions are crucial to building a happy future for the community. This fundamental concern makes the book a revealing one for African Americans. I am not trying to incite revolt, separation, or frustration. My role is that of a whistle blower, appealing to our conscience about the black community's current situation which, in my opinion, deserves better.

This difficult situation has lasted too long. I had the vision of talking about the spiritual axes affecting my cousins' lives. And as such, it is important that I not just remain a critic, an analyst of the situation. But that I also suggest an alternative proposal, able to provide new parameters that can take my cousins, my brothers, out of their current living conditions. What I have been demonstrating from the beginning is a resolution tool by which I wish to offer the African American community a chance to remove the stigma period it has been going through.

I am writing this book to make a necessary contribution to raise the lives of my American cousins, whose parents lived through one of the greatest crimes committed against humanity. This awareness-raising book also aims at making them firmly committed to improving their own lives. That is my vision, and that is why I speak in this chapter of a reunification of my successful brothers who have an enviable social position. They are currently only a minority within the community; and the problem is about the majority who are suffering and in need of help.

This majority needs their union and solidarity to make it as well. It is the vision, the proposal presented here, which is by no means an imposition at the expense of those who have had the merit of being successful.

CHAPTER IX

THE EYE OF THE RETURN

There have been some programs in the past to help descendants of former slaves return to their homelands, particularly in Liberia and Sierra Leone.

After the independence of Africa, Ghana, under the initiative of the late President Kwame Nkrumah, was the first former slave-selling country which opened its doors for the return of our American cousins. There were even talks about allocating land to any descendant of slaves who would have established his Ghanaian origins through a DNA test. As of today, that initiative has helped about 2,500 African Americans return to Ghana.

According to history, more than 15 million people were taken from Africa to build the so-called rich countries. The number of returns, thanks to Ghana's initiative, represents virtually nothing compared to what has been taken from Africa.

Other countries, such as Senegal, have also taken various initiatives in this direction.

The late President, Mathieu KEREKOU of Benin, and his government in the 2000s, had initiated an annual International Festival of Gospel and Roots to encourage African Americans to visit their homeland, Benin. This cultural and historical event aimed at a return to the roots, and a reconnection between the children of the long-gone brothers and Africa, their homeland.

This return trip to Africa was the fulfillment of a precious dream for many people torn from their origin.

One of my clients in Washington, D.C., once told me that after the abolition of slavery, at Inkwell Martha's Vineyard, slaves built a wall on the coast that they climbed from time to time. They did this just to try to see from afar where they came from, for lacking the possibility to physically go there. The intense desire to return home after being released and freed could not be satisfied. The slavery curse and spiritual blockage did not allow the former slaves and their descendants to take advantage of their freedom to return home.

Many of the former slaves had the great desire to leave the land which was associated with the hell they had been through and return home to trace their story. The initiatives of Ghana, Benin, Senegal, and other countries should of course be opportunities to be grasped as part of the dream to return home. But after slavery ended, new blockages appeared to complicate the slaves' dream to return to their forefathers' land. We'll come back to that.

Will my American cousins ever be able to return home though? No one can answer with certainty. Apart from spiritual obstacles, even from a physical point of view, it is now clear that the slaves' descendants are in another vision of the life. Since slavery was abolished more than a century ago, the various attempts to return to Africa have been rather timid. The experience aforementioned from Ghana, simply indicates that this return project has not yet gained importance in the hearts of the descendants of the slaves. The slave will not return so easily to the origin land of his ancestors.

A lot has changed in my cousins' lives. From a cultural point of view for instance, they will not feel at home in some way. They now have a different vision, their current mentality is not compatible with that of African societies, and the levels of maturity are not the same. The way in which black Americans have been raised for example, will make the African society reject them. The food they consume for their physical growth and sustenance is different from African dishes. So much has changed that even though the desire to return remains obvious, it is non-motivating factors that may always keep them away from their origin.

Limited resources are also an obstacle to fulfilling the wishes of many people who really want to know where they come from.

Africa is in fact, very far away from their country and the journey is expensive. No measures are implemented to help them discover the splendor and beauty of Africa, their mother and mother of humanity. It is extremely sad and almost a torment to feel a desire of such intensity, and not be able to satisfy it before dying.

It is a fact that my cousins are no longer the same people as when they were sold. They have changed; they now have this personality that we all seek to understand. They are not the ones who were sold and taken away, but their descendants. They have acquired a freedom that they really want to enjoy. They are no longer the same people in their black skin; their blood has been transformed and mixed. In Africa's eyes, they remain lost children.

Slaves change dimensions from generation to generation, especially when they are freed. They will not systematically consider returning to their homeland. It has been proven that slaves generally often fail to return their homeland. Their land of departure is often seen as a land of misfortune, and most of all as a land that had rejected them. Thus, they no longer seek to see their land of origin just for spiritual reasons. Or, if they try to return, it could be an experience made of many ups and downs, and often with no way out. The Bible, in the book of Exodus, tells us that when the people of Israel were liberated, they took the direction of a new promised land. And even then, God took forty years to wipe out all those who left Egypt. They all died in the wilderness, including their liberating guide, Moses, before the path to the new destination was shown to the new generation born from the few deemed capable of resuming a new life. This is not just a biblical story studied in theology or preached to encourage Christians. What happened in Israel then was purely spiritual because God knows what becomes of a slave's mentality. He knows what becomes of a slave after his liberation. A new land and a new generation purified from the curse of slavery were needed to create a better life for the descendants of those who were enslaved.

This is what Israel experienced in the harshest suffering across the desert. African Americans' desert is still here and has nothing in common with that of the children of Israel. My cousins' desert is still intact, has never been crossed, and their purification never took place. Not only is the curse of slavery still in effect, but the occult programmed in the slaves' spiritual system before they left also prevents their descendants from contemplating a return. Crossing the door of no return or going through the rituals around the fetish tree, for example.

At least the children of Israel knew their God and worshipped Him. Most of my cousins, whether in Africa or America, to this day still don't have a clear idea of their own God or don't really know Him. So, there is like a mixture in their spiritual life, which in itself creates other forms of complications. My American cousins found themselves in a world that doesn't benefit them. Their true liberation could not have been initiated by the white folks who only exploited them, but rather by their homeland which sent them into perdition.

The return of my cousins to Africa will not be easy until further notice. In view of current realities, such a return should be delayed or even better thought through. The world is indeed changing, but traces of the curse remain. These are reflected in some African American businesses. The slave has been uprooted; he lost touch with his origins. He has been rejected; rejected by his own, by those who sold him and who do not expect his return. The slave is seen as an enemy by his origin. He is sometimes the subject of negative decisions by the government of his original land, or there are few measures promoting his return. It, therefore, wouldn't be easy for him to go back because his steps were immediately erased after his departure. On the other hand, even the slave's mind must be reformatted; he who only craved freedom. The need to return now arises together with a great psycho-mental problem in the Afro-Americans' lives. Many questions, therefore, remain mostly unanswered. The accumulation of unanswered questions leads to increased frustrations, a source of revolt on all fronts. And revolt, fed by unanswered questions, only pushes my cousins further into an evil and vicious circle which was thought to be over; that of the slave in slave ties.

This is the reason for my efforts today. To help my African American cousins find a way out, find their spiritual liberation. This mission feels heavy; and in my heart, through my writings, it is as if I will be out of breath. Understanding such a complex situation and managing to put in place an honorable exit plan is indeed quite difficult.

That is why I feel the weight of the commitment I have freely made. Whenever I must deal with a chapter in this book, I discover more things that history itself cannot explain. Solving the slavery puzzle and going back to the axes of the freedom of souls once converted into slaves is profound. The present imposes itself with its reality, the future does not even want to deal with the present, and the past dictates its law, making the present difficult. I feel within me the duty to reveal over and over again, this thing hidden in them, eating away at them every moment of their lives. I feel all alone on this path without an Aaron, who at least accompanied Moses every time he visited Pharaoh. I have no Joshua waiting to act as the leader, so as to show the way after the release of this book. Like Moses, I only have my spiritual rod to help my cousins realize that they have a spiritual problem that must be solved first. I have God building me up with his spirit and through these writings. I am fully certain that a vital change will occur in the lives of those who would have understood everything I demonstrate and denounce in this book.

The deep trauma suffered by my cousins reappears today. It is more difficult to bear because they were unknown in the past, but now revealed. They were just told that their great-grandparents were slaves. History withheld information all because no one cares about the life led by my dear African American cousins. Under these circumstances, a definitive, organized return to their original land is not immediately possible. There are still so many barriers to understand and overcome.

However, knowledge of the past is coming to light. A visit to the African American Museum in Washington, D.C., gives one a glimpse into the huge impact left by the small country I come from. The museum speaks of Dahomeans kings, and one cannot evoke African American history without mentioning that kingdom. In the previous chapters, I shed some light on provisions that were made by DAHOMEY before sending the slaves away. Your surprise will be even greater when you discover one of the powerful instruments used during the reign of King AGADJA, initiator of the tree of oblivion.

"Let's send them away without them being able to retrace their steps because everything has been erased from their memory. But let's grant their souls a return to the land of their forefathers..."

These are probably the kind of words said during the discussions that led to the decision on the measures to be taken before the slave expedition by King AGADJA and his royal court. It was then that another fetish tree was established in 1727, which would be called "The Tree of the Return", a tree with its own spiritual function. Unlike the tree of oblivion, it would allow the souls of slaves to return to their homeland only after their death. This meant that the slaves leaving Benin (DAHOMEY at the time), were not to return to their homeland until they were dead. The return tree was a fetish tree that served as a landmark antenna for the souls of slaves who died in the land of the white folks. It was then mandatory that all slaves, after being stripped of their memory, to go around this fetish tree three times, both men and women. All this was done in the presence of the divinity EGOUNGOUN, which is the divinity of spirit of death.

That again is a sickening measure taken by our forefathers who were making sure that the slaves would never return to their homeland alive. It is important for us to understand today, that these provisions should not be overlooked or treated lightly in the lives of black people. The desire to return to their land of origin is evident in most black folks, but is suppressed, or its fulfilment prevented by something. The desire to leave everything behind to return to their forefathers, because of a system which does not favor them, naturally manifests itself in Afro-Americans. But it is as though there will never be a way to fulfill this legitimate desire. Have you ever wondered why the financial resources to prepare for a return seem to lack? Why the black people feel so financially limited to undertake their return? Or even why, despite their wealth, some slave descendants, don't even think about visiting their fathers land?

Have you wondered why, despite the advanced technology that allows flights to land in Africa in less than twelve hours, no definitive return is organized? Have you tried to understand why DJIMON HOUNSOU, famous Benin-born actor and American citizen, can go to the land of his ancestors and spend all the time he wants without a problem? Have you tried to find out why AKON, the American Singer from Senegal, with Goree island being the crossroads for dispatching slaves, can return to the land of his ancestors, stay there, and enjoy it as he pleases?

For the slaves, the decision was made that only their souls will return to Africa. There is the blockage, simply put. Everything is spiritually controlled in the lives of the slaves' descendants; and there has been no proper correction to date. I should reiterate, however, that the tree of the return of the soul did not start operating until the year 1727. This means that not all slaves went through it; but even those who have gone before it, have not always returned. Let us remember once again that the curse is contagious through the blood. And by that, I mean through the bonds of marriage, sex, friction, and the environment. It was in a way this kind of promiscuous contagion that the indefensible Jim Crow laws tried to avoid.

The tree of the return, yet another divinity that comes into play in the analysis and understanding of what African Americans are going through. Why then were all these arrangements made?

The African kingdoms, before the invasion of the white human traffickers and then colonizers, were organized kingdoms, as I said at the beginning of this book. The royal palace was very structured and made ministerial arrangements; ministers with well-defined portfolios were appointed. In all circumstances, a minister of worship remained in place and was directly linked to the royal palace. The king consulted the ancestors and spirits all the time for good governance. The oracles and divinities, were then, regularly consulted. In that context, a possible return of the slaves could have been predicted by the occult priest through the Fâ, Oracle, an instrument of communication between men and future. The oracle is a science used to predict the future. The oracle could have predicted a possible return of the slaves, which would have been perceived as a real danger to the entire population left behind. The oracle could have already signaled the creation of Liberia to the King, who would have taken immediate measures to avoid such a situation. In other words, the eventual return of the slaves or their descendants to the land of origin would have been a real threat. A great disaster to the natives; for they would come back with a different spirit, a different mentality, and a new intelligence that could have made life difficult for the people there. It was, therefore, best that they never retraced their steps back. That only their souls were allowed to return to the land of their ancestors.

This in my view, was just a precautionary measure which, in fact, should not be misunderstood or taken in a negative sense. The measure against their eventual return was a way of preserving the future of the local population, which was to be preserved in case those who left ever decided to return.

Let's imagine for a moment that African Americans were now massively returning to Africa. What would have been Africa's fate if there had been an immediate return of freed slaves in the aftermath of the abolition? Let's try an analysis of conscience that allows us to come up with a solution. From these reflections, it seems that a return can only be planned after a certain path. For example, when the descendants of the slaves have regained their state of consciousness and morality, when they have rid themselves of all grudges and bitterness. It is more or less a long process of healing, liberation, or even forgiveness and reconciliation. No one can agree with what has been done, the negative measures that have been taken. But one can understand and explain the reasons for all these occult provisions of the past, which still penalize most of my cousins today.

In our ancestors' defense, during the consultations of the oracle, great threats against the people of AGADJA in the event of the return of the slaves they were selling, could have been predicted. No one knew how long the buyers or masters were going to keep the slaves. Everyone was aware of the physical capacity of these slaves, who could at any moment provoke a rebellion and an uprising, killing their masters along the way and returning back to the kingdom. The chances and the risks were high. The oracle could have signaled the danger even outside any king's consultation as a warning. Everything had been established spiritually. Nothing was randomly done. Good governance requires a good king to protect his people; and if the ancestors and spirits had ever challenged him about the safety of the people, there would have been nothing to do but take the appropriate measures.

Today, unfortunately, on one side there are victims and banished, and on the other there are preserved and protected because of these measures which have been taken and which have left a lot of harm without reparation. I will stick to my main goal, which is to propose solutions, and promote hope in my African American cousins' community. I will avoid any confusion or contradiction in this chapter that might lead to a misunderstanding of my ideas. But I would at the same time like to observe the provisions of King AGADJA with an open mind. To understand that these measures, at that time, were positive for some and negative for others. Only their souls would return, following the direction antenna which is nothing but the tree of the return.

The arrangement of the return tree does not, of course, promote the kind of burning desire the Massachusetts slaves, already mentioned above, felt about returning to their homeland. This desire will push them to build a wall from which they looked from afar beyond the vast ocean at Inkwell Martha's Vineyard. All this because the oracle would have, in the meantime, revealed to AGADJA what could later happen to the Liberia natives following the return of freed slaves from America.

Remember that around 1822, a little over eleven thousand descendants of slaves returned to the West African coast. They named the land which welcomed them Liberia, then gained independence in 1847 from the United States, their masters' country. From then on, the freed slaves found themselves in the master's shoes, thanks to their new knowledge. Behaving as such, they were able to impose themselves on the Aboriginal people who were present before their arrival. Let's analyze the logic of the measures which were taken based on the real history of Liberia. This is surely the kind of revelation King AGADJA would have received long before the Fa's revelation, which would have led him to take the steps he deemed useful to preserve his people.

Freed slaves returned to what was considered the land of their ancestors. Once they got there, they took charge and ruled the natives; the very ones who were actually the landowners. The returned slaves' descendants' behavior was not limited to just creating the Republic of Liberia. The new country's constitution and management bodies were modeled on their former masters' country, the United States of America. Even Liberia's national flag is almost a copy of the American flag, with one star instead fifty. The former slaves and their descendants who returned, unceremoniously dominated for more than a century the indigenous people who remained in Africa and did nothing to improve their living conditions. What a turnaround! This example, which I discovered during my research, clearly shows that the slaves who became masters on their ancestors' land, had acquired a completely different mentality, a different education. Once they returned to Africa, they lived and behaved like their masters whom they left. They established the same arrangements the masters had made against them, such as the deprivation of the right to vote, the separation of clans, and the denial of citizenship.

In some places, those who returned even went so far as to sell black natives to whites who came to buy them. Others rejected African traditions or made life hell for the people who welcomed them, opened their arms, and offered them a place to live like their lost and returned children. How frustrating and upsetting it might have been to watch slaves, who went through hell under white folks, be incapable of elevating their state of consciousness to the point of never putting their own brother of the same skin color through the same horrible conditions. They otherwise became slave traders too. Slaves subjugating slaves, slaves selling slaves. What an aberration!

*This is the representation of **"The Tree of Return"** to which the slaves should turn around three times so that their spirit can return to the original land after their death.*

The Spirit Behind The Wall

Egungun is the Vodou of the spirit of the dead. This is a statuette of the Egungun which is the Vodou in the presence of which the slaves must perform their ritual of return.

The divinely informed King AGADJA, therefore, had to preserve his kingdom, DAHOMEY, from this eventual return; for the oracle had predicted it. It was necessary to take immediate measures to ensure that it did not happen; that was his role as king.

In the example mentioned above, for more than a century, the founders of Liberian, slaves who returned to Africa, who dressed and ate like their white masters, mistreated Africans as they pleased. They rejected the natives' language, forced them to speak English, and imposed Christianity as the best religion. These obvious antagonisms created deeper problems of social cohesion. That's when I realized that the solution wasn't as simple as I envisioned it. It was not just a matter of helping my black American cousins overcome the obstacles preventing their return to Africa, but the solution today is more complex in view of the examples previously mentioned. We also must look at the wounds of the Liberian natives, and others, to see if King AGADJA was right or wrong to take the various fetish measures to prevent the freed slaves' incredible behavior. I meditate and look from a distance at the tree of oblivion and the tree of the return to mature my thoughts on the Afro-Americans' lives, on what they've been through, and what will become of them when the final solution is found.

Similarly, what will become of Africa if African Americans ever regain their spirit and return? What will be the fate of Africans in their hands when they resettle one day on the land of their forefathers? In fact, the behavior is in the blood; it is transmitted. The wrath of the slaves' ancestors and their spirit of vengeance are silently passed down from generation to generation. The example of what happened in Liberia shows that resentment is still present in the blood of slaves' descendants. That is where the problem lies. Many of my cousins are filled with the spirit of revenge and resentment, even though it is not too blatant. The trauma is deep; long, tedious work will be required to prepare the spirits for forgiveness and reconciliation.

Having said that, our ancestors should not have sold their brothers away in the first place; let alone having to take these unfortunate measures and precautions.

There has not been a massive comeback in recent history. The return project still hasn't picked up. Even though some three thousand slaves' descendants are settled in Ghana today, we cannot really speak of a mass return. A lot has changed in the people's lives on both sides; hence, the need to carefully prepare the process on all sides. Heal past and present blockages; remove suspicions and restore mutual trust and consideration. Ensure mutual acceptance and relearn to live together in a spirit of solidarity and complementarity; establish a whole recovery process.

A whole process of restoration and broken spiritual, socio-cultural, economic, and political links. Despite the urgency, nothing so complex and beautiful can be accomplished in haste and unpreparedness. The return project still has a bright future ahead of it. There is hope since the will to reunite exists and is developing on both sides.

On one hand, the flame of the desire to return to Africa remains lit within the black American community and their leaders. This is evidenced by the proliferation of movements and associations interested in Africa (historical or religious "Root" pilgrimages, cultural tourism, business or study trips, literary publications, lobbying for Africa, etc.).

On the other hand, the commemoration of events related to the history of slavery, the erection of monuments of remembrance, the call for the return of the diaspora, the promotion of reconnection activities, the designation by the African Union of the Diaspora as a "geographic region" of the continent, etc.

A whole process is underway, which to succeed must not neglect the important aspect of spiritual healing.

CHAPTER X

THE CURSE OF THE NAME

A curse can, in general, be defined as words by which one wishes someone a harmful fate; but it can be cancelled. There are indeed solutions in every belief system to stop a curse whatever its nature, although some are more difficult to stop than others. If I told you that George Washington was an African American, many of you would call me crazy; yet the truth is that George Washington was the name given to a slave's descendant. Born in Diamond, MO, to Giles and Mary Carver, George Washington was a botanist inventor. He died in January 1943 in Tuskegee near Atlanta. This may seem ironic to you, but a black man once bore the name G. W., the same name as that of the first president of the United States of America. This shows how strongly the slave ancestors felt about seeing their descendants become masters and authority figures in this country for which they shed their blood. Their desire not to see their descendants fall into the situation we deplore today must also have been strong. Naturally, every parent wishes their children the very best. George Washington, the botanist inventor of the method of self-prevention's, full name was George Washington Carver. Some parents used the name trick to change their descendants' fate or forever erase the serial number with which their ancestors set foot on American soil.

Let's not forget that back then, after the slaves were auctioned in Africa, they were taken into rooms where they were marked according to their slave trafficker. They were given a serial number; their names were systematically erased. Those human beings became the traders' properties and they carried serial numbers as if they were no longer humans, but like a license plate to cars nowadays. They did not leave Africa with their original name, but with identification numbers such as cattle. Also remember the Black Code promulgated by Louis XIV, King of France.

In Africa, we often come across family names like Do-Rego, Da-Silva, Do-Santos, De-Souza, Domingo, etc. These names often refer to slaves belonging to the masters bearing them. The particle Do, Da or De, often means "for". So, for example De-Rego would mean Rego's slave. These names are sometimes also attributed to certain slaves that the traders bought and exploited locally. This would mean that some slaves stayed in Africa to serve their white masters and, therefore, did not lose their roots, or their source; but still had the blood of a slave.

Meanwhile, the vast majority of the slaves were transported out of Africa. Those were the ones who were registered, had identification numbers, lost human value, and were given the status of an object and servitude.

The name just like the blood, has a great spiritual value in an individual's life, and together they can define the future. As we see in the Bible, the Supreme God changed many people's names. For example, Jacob became Israel so that he could prosper, otherwise, he was in bondage (Genesis 32: 25-29). Sarai, Abraham's wife, became Sarah which means princess before she could conceive. Abram became Abraham so that the establishment of God's covenant with his people could be fulfilled (Genesis 17: 1-5; 15). So that Joseph could rule Egypt, Pharaoh will change his name and call him "Tsaphnath Paeneach" (Genesis 41:45). The name is like the soul's reference that can easily give access to the spirit. According to well-established practices in some societies, a sorcerer can bewitch or heal a person by simply calling their name. The name one bears is a spiritual organ of communication with the mind and soul that can represent the individual everywhere. Saying a name can attract unhappiness or happiness. By your name you can prove to be a builder or a loser.

The slaves' name was not a source of happiness, rather another cause of condemnation for their descendants. That may well be the reason for the deplorable state in which they are now. One wonders how someone who was long defined by a sales or purchase registration, could suddenly experience happiness without having previously experienced a real deliverance. During my training as an evangelist, we were taught a chapter on deliverance. That class covered all kinds of deliverance methods, often referring to the blood and name. We had a class on deliverance of the blood and soul, but also one on the deliverance of the name. The misfortune did not stop at the conversion of their noble blood of worthy sons of Africa into a slaves' blood. The curse didn't only stem from the occult practices used by our ancestors to convert them to a lower status individual. The problem that is passed down from generation to generation not only builds on the spirit of bondage, but also the name by which these brave children of Africa were referred to. The slaves, who were heroes, never experienced the cold of winter in Africa; but still survived it in their dormitory without a heating system in America.

The history today seems to ignore all these tragedies and their spiritual impact on the lives of the African American descendants. They are required to lead a noble life, which they are not yet capable of.

The curse of the name is one of the facts that secretly paralyze the African American descendants who, despite being liberated more than a century ago, still live as if they were submissive. In reality, their minds and blood are still not free. The spirit always remembers the old name, and the old name or registration, dictates to the blood and soul a way of life contrary to what my cousins would have liked. Today, there is a conflict of identity because of the name. They are called by a name which is contrary to what it was. There is some sort of battle of a spiritual identity within, a confusion of the source of the personality, a stifling of the will to succeed, and above all, the absence of a sense of pride due to the fact that they bear the name of the former master. Many people in the Afro-American communities, without a doubt, have a lot of questions about their lives because they don't really understand what's happening to them.

The name one bears dictates its law, the blood that circulates in one's veins dictates its law. This causes the confusion that is the reason for the absence of identity; for it is difficult for one to settle and properly respond to these multiple influences. Under such pressure, one finds it difficult to remain conscious. It becomes easier to give into temptations, indulge in drugs, or surrender to alcohol; just to forget about the hardships, to feel a bit better in one's head. The mind is thus manipulated inside the body with the black skin. The body is trampled by the many pre-established provisions that existed before the abolition of slavery. Can we ever talk about the liberation of the slave's spirit so that his life gets better? This, of course, is not good news to the former masters' descendants. Ending slavery did not happen out of love, or by coercion, or even because of a fight unleashed by slaves who escaped the masters' whip and became aware of the freedom necessary for their future generation. It was rather, a matter of taking a qualitative leap towards the construction of the new world.

Abolition was proclaimed; doors were opened to the establishment of a new system, another dimension. The segregation system then took place, and it was the beginning of another struggle, not the end. Civil rights will be granted to black people not because they were entitled to them, but because it suited some former masters, who took the time to study things well. They were convinced that the slaves would never be able to use these rights to change their future. What good can civil rights do today if one wanders from dawn to dusk in crossroads or on the streets without employment or food? Often under the influence of drugs and alcohol. What is the point of holding a citizenship if one's access to education is compromised? It has all been manipulated for so long! It's now time to understand this and wake up from the general paralysis created by the opposite force.

Worthless names, names with no nobility, names with no respect, were attributed to slaves after removing the registration they brought from Africa. They were called savages, for example, and they were treated that way. Thinking about this makes me pause, sigh, so as to recover from the great internal pain I feel. My eyes have dried out, I have no more tears right now. My heart refuses to let go because it is aware of my mission to the cousins. My fingers continue writing a version of slavery that has been hidden all this time from them. Migraines run through my head; it hurts to get into the skin of my African American cousins and live what they go through; even for a few seconds. I refuse to accept what I am writing, but the source of my inspiration, being divine, imposes it on me and I have no other choice but to take it out and experience this internal pain. It's as if a spirit dictates everything I write, a spirit that prevents me from stopping until everything that comes to my mind is all courageously transcribed. And when my soul starts crying out, I feel the emotional pain. I feel the need to be resuscitated because I burn with emotion. The lives of the slaves have been transformed as if they had gone through mechanical processes of transformation.

The "savage" has been trained with wickedness by a race; his name was changed because it was seen as a domestic or docile animal. The gaze of these slaves towards their distant origin will be extinguished like an oil-hungry lantern. We are talking about three hundred years of pain, suffering, transformation, and torture mechanisms. Nothing can repair such profound harm; but perhaps simple forgiveness suffices.

The names my cousins bear today must be analyzed to better know their meaning. The black American, in this context, actually has no real family, having lost the traces of his ancestors. In Africa, one can generally identify one's lineage with the family. One knows your ethnicity just by hearing your name. Your nobility, your dignity is identified just by your name. My cousins have none of that anymore, because for a long time they answered to serial numbers. They were labeled before they were given a name; a tactic to define them as savages and property.

My other observation is that at every Thanksgiving commemoration where every family gets together, when you ask my cousins where they will go to celebrate, most of them say, *"nowhere"*. Others are often indifferent, choosing instead to remember the death of their ancestors. All the family traces are blurred by the frequent name changes, all landmarks lost. What is more disgusting is the possible inbred marriages contracted out of ignorance. Unfortunately, these are common cases in the black community because they do not know each other. We cannot condemn them about this, but we can change it all, and this change will come from us.

Despite their difficult living conditions, many black people have come up with great scientific inventions. But the system has done everything to ensure that their names do not appear anywhere. They could not be famous, their names were muffled, those names were considered only slaves condemned to bondage. Many slaves and their descendants contributed to the modernization but were not acknowledged. On the contrary, the glory that could encourage future generations today was stolen from them. I take this opportunity to pay a vibrant tribute to the great afro men and women for having proved that there is much value in the black skin. To all the slaves who left the African coasts, I also pay a public tribute. We may never know your names, but your memory will never be erased. It is forever engraved in our collective consciousness.

Since the name is always of a spiritual value, it is necessary to recognize this value in order to work on it for a possible liberation. Even in Africa, people bear names without knowing their meaning or spiritual value. Many are thus condemned to limitations in their lives, especially with regards to the success or prosperity which they could access.

The same is true in the United States of America, where the situation is even more serious. The family names here generally carry the mark of slavery, and many African Americans bear those names. Hence, the need to awaken everyone's conscience so that the appropriate corrections can be made from birth.

Think about it: OBAMA, a name of value and nobility, which Michelle did not hesitate to bear, because the man who carries it exudes human values. Barack received certain values and qualities from his origin, which one way or another, transferred the know how to him. You are the image of the name you carry in most cases. At the mention of the Obama name, the image of this exemplary first family and the first black president of the United States of America comes to everyone's mind. The same way George Washington Carver's parents, knowing all that their folks went through during their time, decided to name their son G.W. The mere mention of that name, they said, appealed to the value of the great man who was the first American president. Truly, they were calling success, a great personality, and respect from others into their son's existence. It is totally normal that their child went on to become a great inventor bearing his great name: George Washington.

When it comes to one's name, two influences are in play that come from different sources. First, the family name which defines the root, lineage, and fate or future according to the family one comes from. This is very important because each family name has a spiritual marker that generally influences the lives of the children with that name. The second source of influence is one's given name by which one is called daily. This defines one as good or bad and can also define several aspects of one's success. It is, therefore, important to understand today that most black folks did not have a name that would help them succeed, rather one which would make them keep serving the master.

So, what did the names given to the slaves mean and what kind of influences could these have had on the lives of the younger generations today? Every Afro-American should do extensive research about the name they carry, as they try to know their origins through DNA tests. It is important for them to find their name's meaning, why their ancestors carried that name. The results of such research would go a long way in resolving several persistent conflicts in the lives of many.

CHAPTER XI

THE BLACK PEOPLE'S HIDDEN VALUE

Someone once told me during my research for this book that, *"If African Americans were sold, bought, brought to a country unknown to them; survived despite all the suffering they were inflicted, have their spirit in the dark, and still continue to survive despite everything; it means their inner being is endowed with something special. Resistance that they must find in order to afford a better life."*

Even if the election of Barack Obama is not yet the fulfillment of Dr. Martin Luther King Jr.'s dream, it remains a symbol of hope for black people around the world. In that we understand that being black is not a fatality; being black is not accepting a fate that denies life its true value. President Obama's election, especially his management and his unifying heart, prove that the black race is of a surprising quality; with undoubtfully the capacity to build a quality world. Objectively, it would be difficult to judge the Obama couple as evil. This couple showed that within the black skin, are love, respect, intelligence, and a sense of peace. They proved that the black man is not an animal that comes after humans to devour them. We have a great illustration in Barack and Michelle OBAMA. That should now motivate us to know that we, black people whether African, African American, or from anywhere for that matter, can do anything. *"Yes, we can!"* to paraphrase Barak Obama's slogan during his 2008 election campaign.

Developed countries would not be what they are without Africa. Europe or America could not be mentioned without reference to Africans. The great powers of the world, as they like to call themselves, have not reached this level without Africa.

Therefore, we must understand that the black race makes the world happy; and recognize that the real man is not the rich, but the one who has wisdom and shares all that he has, even at his own expense. That is why, African American brothers and cousins, it is now essential to get rid of your weapons of anger provided by injustices and bitterness. It's time to take the time to value the extraordinary quality in you. Now is not the time to remain overwhelmed by the evil of the past which prevents you from actually seeing who you are. The time is to remind you of the late Martin Luther King Jr., who asked all to respond to any provocation with love. Start answering with love and find out who you really are.

Michelle Obama, in one of her campaign speeches, mentioned that the White House was built by slaves. It was not a simple election statement, but a great affirmation of who black people can be. Out of black hands came a white building that houses presidents. Out of the black skin came the intelligence that allowed the construction of a building, loaded with symbols that attracts thousands of people from all over the world. So, we, Africans or African Americans, need to understand that we have something that others do not. The White House alone is enough to make African Americans see the value in them. The Capitol Hill monument is also enough to know who you are and reject what others want you to be. Look at the White House, Capitol Hill, and many other buildings in Washington, D.C., and realize that your value is great and incomparable. Look at the White House and know that there is something pure and bright in you that can make you better than you are now.

The path to take is simple but difficult to choose. Your value is not who you think you are today, who you really are is not yet manifested. Today, a reference is signaled to you every time the sun rises over the White House on Capitol Hill. Know that your talent is bigger than these monuments and whiter than snow. So, set aside the anger that comes from the painful memories, according to which your ancestors who built these monuments were never paid for their labor. Forget the shameless acts of exploitation that naturally stirs revolt in you; and fight to raise yourself to positions that will lead you to enjoy the life your ancestors did not have the opportunity to enjoy.

In fact, there's a secret in you that you don't know about. Your ancestors may not have been able to leave you with the traces of your origin, but they have left silent landmarks that must remind you every day that this world is nothing without the black race, without you. The dance rhythm must change from now on. Your daily life should no longer be made of drugs, cigarettes, alcoholic or adulterated beverages, junk foods, violence, prison, prostitution, resignation, despair, hatred, laziness, abandonment, etc. Your eyes should no longer be focused on horizons of despair; but rather from afar or close on the Nation's Capital, Washington, D.C., at sunrise and tell yourself with conviction that the blood of your fathers built a beautiful life in a beautiful city.

Your priceless value has been hidden from you far too long, dear American cousins. To the point where you stop believing in yourself by ignoring your worth. You gave up, abdicated, refused to trust in yourself, and your own future. Unfortunately, you agreed to take a dead-end path, and sink into it every day. What a tragedy! Yet, many glorious examples are before you! Barack and Michelle Obama, Martin Luther King Jr., Malcolm X, Muhammad Ali, Mae Carol Jemison, Ruby Nell Bridges, Bessie Coleman, Frederick Douglass, Rosa Parks, etc.; to name but a few. You must find courage in remembering them as your ancestors who heroically shed their blood for the American nation. It is up to you to honor them by rejecting any spiritual prison that seeks to seize your unquestionable value in all areas.

In the world of sports, cultural, and recreational activities, there are many black athletes, artists, etc. who has left their mark on football, basketball, the music industry, etc. However, many have yet to be discovered. Some are in jail; others die because of the alcohol, and in the ghettos, in the streets they kill each other, etc.

Beyond the United States of America, black folks from all walks of life need to know that they are among the great achievements of this world. Their blood, and the blood of their ancestors, gave beauty to many nations which enjoy it today. France could never talk about world wars or soccer, without remembering Africans. French medicine, thanks to Bertin Nahum, an African from Benin, has robots that can conduct complex brain surgeries. These few glorious examples should influence our minds, by reminding us that we have great values within the black race and in our communities.

When it comes to education, we talk about the hidden value of black people just because they are intimidated. They have, in general, been convinced to believe that they cannot go further than high school. College tuition is expensive to control their talents. My cousins have been suffocated from the beginning because the master is aware of the slave's potential. Note that the maneuver is common with regards to Black Africans and African Americans. Manipulations and financial pressures are used to deflect black talents from the right path in order to prevent them from one day being able to switch places with the former master.

CHAPTER XII

THE BREAD OF RESPONSIBILITY

The fate of the slaves' descendants is the real topic right now. It is my book's landmark and the knot that must be untied to let my black cousins live in the proper world's vision. Thus, it is important to get the true facts out in order to end a problem. Responsibilities must be set for what needs to be done to be accomplished. I categorize these responsibilities in three points. Again, I am not trying to accuse or blame, anyone, any race, or country. My humble opinion is that we must all (black and white alike) take responsibility for the evil that has been done, for this common sin. To simply accept this in order to better understand my demonstration in the remainder of this chapter. Three channels in the inhuman slaves' trade since the beginning of this book: white human traffickers, the sellers, and the slaves. They all have a great deal of responsibility in the lives of the African Americans, so let's determine each party's fault.

THE WHITE SLAVE TRADERS:

In this group, there were the traders and the slaves' owners.

The traders:

They went to Africa to buy the slaves and sell them in America or other places in the world. The descendants of those merchants must understand that they enjoy a legacy based on human trade, with all the abuses that surrounded it. It is important for them to do themselves a favor by paying some dues out of their inheritance, even if they believe that they owe nothing to the descendants of the slaves. How should they go about this? They owe huge repairs to my cousins; and must recognize the harm done to black folks (Africans and African Americans) via a sincere mea culpa. The traders' descendants need to understand that in trying to right the wrongs done, they free themselves and future generation from a very heavy karma. They avoid incurable diseases in the sense that they spare themselves, as much as younger generations, unexplainable sufferings. It is extremely important that they find ways and means for a solemn reparation so that the suffering party releases them. I am saying: *"acknowledge your wrongdoings and release yourself; repair the evil, which was done, and free yourself. Go beyond your mind to understand and sympathize with the suffering of black folks, and your blood will also be cleaned of the dark loads that you ignore."*

The slaves' owners:

When I mentioned incurable diseases regarding the traders earlier, it is the same and worse for the descendants of the slaves' owners. Today, retirement homes are filled with white people wasting away in their beds alive. Many suffer from cancers or diseases unexplainable by medicine. This is all karmic. The slaves' owners' descendants must revise their history and change ideas about black people; in their case, even a mea culpa will not be enough. A monument itself will not repair the wrong that has been done. The African American History Museum in Washington, D.C., is not enough to extinguish the painful flame felt by the slaves' descendants. We need way more than what has been already done. I think that the system needs to be overhauled for African Americans to find their way back to life. When I talk about the system, I mean everything, visible and invisible, that is penalizing and preventing black Americans from succeeding and prospering. That in which limits them to a life that gives them no choice. The United States of America is still run by the descendants of former slaves' owners. How does a system established even before the end of slavery benefit African Americans? This country's fundamental texts have never been changed, other than the various amendments that have been added. Nothing has been modified with the Afro-Americans' best interests in mind.

I sincerely think that the descendants of the slaves' owners are to start the reparation process there, with the fundamental texts. To consider black folks today is a good start that will give them opportunities for mental and physical liberation. Recognize the wrong your ancestors did and repair their faults. Acknowledgement and repair must go hand in hand at this level. I would even suggest that December 18, the day on which the slavery abolition was effective in the United States of America, be recognized as a memorable and public holiday. This is one of the great recognitions that could be made.

Let the flags be specially flown at half-mast to ask African Americans for their forgiveness annually for the wrong of the past. The responsibilities of the descendants of the slaves' owners are enormous, in my opinion, but this book is only talking about peace and solutions. I would not want to awaken the minds of my cousins on things that could lead to anger and violent reactions.

The descendants of the sellers:

On November 28, 2017, during a meeting with students in Ouagadougou, Burkina Faso, the French President Macron, responded this to a young student concerned about the slavery situation in Libya. *"Tell me, who are the ones selling slaves in Libya? It is not the French or the Belgians or the Americans; it is the Africans…"*

This President had no reservations about saying it out loud, for it was the pure indisputable truth. The same question also arises about the slave trade. Africans sold their brothers to white strangers. Like President Macron, we must also admit it out loud; Africa is partly responsible for this trade. This would not have happened without the great dedication of the Africans, who even waged wars and took occult measures to sell their brothers to slave traders.

No resistance has been recorded against the nasty trade proposed by the slave merchants. Africa, who was as innocent as a virgin woman, lost her virginity by her contribution in this business. Nothing had been done to go against it. Africa had the means to refuse and oppose those Europeans traders who had come to buy their brother's blood to build their countries. But instead, our ancestors welcomed them with open arms and offered them their own brother's and children's blood for junk, without any remorse.

It is, therefore, necessary for each party to be truly clear about its responsibilities. So that everyone; seller, buyer, and owner are aware of the damage that was caused. To remedy a situation, one must know its origin. It is human beings we are talking about; beings who were sold like cattle. We are talking about the wrong caused to an entire race. Here, we are looking for those responsible for the hurt caused to the black race. I am fearlessly calling out Africa, our ancestors who showed no love, no mercy towards their own, and I am doing so out loud. Africa is partially responsible for all this evil.

Africa, by its naivety, caused the trouble we see in the black American community today. Africa owes an apology to the children she sold. Some countries are more guilty than others in this slavery case. These countries must be able to take a concrete act of regret towards these cousins of mine. This should not be just a story that is told, or films inspired by a film writer producing a semblance of knowledge. We need concrete actions of resolution from Africa. I am not sure any steps have been taken by my cousins, who are still suffering from the abuses of slavery, in order to understand what they are going through and help themselves. I call on those countries that sold their children and demand physical and spiritual dispositions to open the veils of a definitive liberation of these souls imprisoned for hundreds of years.

Slaves' descendants:

Three college girls on vacation in Washington, D.C., drew my attention to a point I must share with you to talk about my African American cousins regarding their lives. On their way to Chinatown, D.C., for lunch, we passed through H Street, one of the main lanes in front of the White House on the north side. One of them asked the other two to look at the WH; to my surprise, they jointly reacted by saying in unison, *"We don't give a shit about the white house!"* One of them added, *"Our grandparents who built this house were never paid."* They were all desolate and cold after that comment. That immediately changed the atmosphere, and one could feel this heavy grudge and bitterness in those African American girls. Many Afro-Americans are still frustrated by the stories related to everything their grandparents endured.

Even though that is the reality we cannot deny today, it does not have to be a fatality or a reason for demeaning oneself, frustration, or stagnation. All that is important now is that my cousins understand that the irreparable is done and move on. They must take actions to remedy the harm that was done centuries ago. They need to change the way they view this whole topic, so their lives can change.

Now, we must understand that even if the American government decides to compensate the slaves' descendants for all the abuse their forefathers experienced; even if the U.S. government organizes a great mea culpa ceremony, my cousins' lives still will not change in any way. It is sometimes good to review one's position as a victim when reparations are expected. The African Americans responsibility in this evil situation is reflected in their spirit of vengeance and revolt against the white race and Africans. They need stop believing that they have been the victims of injustice without reparation.

No compensation or reparation will fix the African Americans' minds. Only they can work on themselves to get out of the situation that tortures them. I believe that the remedy they hope for must begin with them. The only way to take possession of what is rightfully theirs, is by putting a new mentality in their own minds. *"Succeed to honor the soul of my ancestors,"* should be a good slogan for them.

This is crucial because they are on the wrong path by standing idly by, not wanting to go to school or work. Barack and Michelle Obama would not have been able to spend eight years in the White House if they had not made the decision to live a life different from the one most African Americans lead.

I am asking my African American cousins to search within themselves for a special thing that they can implement, to not only honor their forefathers, but also to gradually address the trauma and change the way they feel. They must find a way to leave the past behind and look forward to building a brighter future. They cannot keep playing the victims for the rest of their lives, from generation to generation. The sentiment of revolt and anger serve them no more; it keeps them in bondage. Slavery has been over for one hundred and fifty years, so they now owe it to themselves to make change as to prosper and to better honor their ancestors.

My dear cousins now must face the situation head on because no one else can do it for them. Come together for a firm resolution and put an end to the evil and trauma it caused. There are many ways to make a wrong right and get reparation. The best way to go about it is to start questioning yourself and display the better side in you, so the other side realizes that they were wrong about yourself. In a country like the United States of America, you must reject poverty and stand up for your future by taking responsibility. Fighting in silence while working on oneself ends injustices and condemnations. I would like to go back in history to appeal to my cousins' conscience in order to make them understand the reasons that should motivate them to take their responsibility.

In June 1944, a young black boy was sentenced to death and executed by the electric chair at more than 5000 volts for a crime he did not commit. Two little white girls, aged seven and eleven, were murdered. George Stinney Jr. was, according to the police, the girls' killer. South Carolina's justice sentenced the fourteen-year-old George to death by the electric chair. Seventy years later (in 2014) his conviction was overturned. George did not have the right lawyer to defend him and Judge Philip H. Stoll who sentenced him was nothing but a former master. According to history, the court didn't want to hear his appeal. Governor Olin D. Johnston of South Carolina denied appeals for clemency on his behalf. My take on this, is that George Stinney Jr. might have had a better chance if had had a black lawyer to defend him.

Back then, segregation was still in full swing. Today, only a radical change of heart will get my cousins out of this mess. A rigorous process of continuous work to heal the wounds they have carried way too long. And again, no apologies or compensation will meet the demands of their bruised hearts. Their responsibility is to start taking their lives seriously, as to make a better future.

Everybody has a share of responsibility in this long-lasting traumatizing situation; may it be the victims, the slave owners, the sellers, or the merchants. But everyone is refusing take responsibility for their share by blaming the others. The traders now say that they have nothing to do with it, and that the Africans willingly delivered their sons to them; they only bought those people. At the same time, Africans feel they have been betrayed by the merchants. The owners on their part, think they have nothing to do with this story because they only bought a commodity that they needed for their business. Next are the victims, looking at the owners and sellers, wanting revenge. All this takes us nowhere of course. Anyone affected by this should start working on his consciousness by accepting his share of responsibility and envisioning the end to this unacceptable suffering.

CHAPTER XIII

THE FLIP SIDE OF SLAVERY IN AFRICA

My maternal grandmother met her father after turning seventeen-years-old. She was already about to get married when her father returned from Abomey, the headquarters of the slave capturing organization. Her father, a dignitary in his village a few kilometers north of Abomey, had been abducted. Her mother was pregnant with her when her father was forced to leave and serve the king as the Fâ high priest. She told us this touching story with great emotion, and we could feel that she missed her father's love. Her distant gaze sometimes showed that she went back in time to relive those painful moments which stayed with her all her life.

Slavery left painful scars in the hearts of many African families. Which today, creates huge ethnic wounds to the point that ethnic groups do not trust each other. I remember my grandmother trying to know my wife's ethnicity; back then, she was my pregnant girlfriend. My grandmother's inquiry was to determine whether she would be a good woman or not. It is a different way for people in Africa to cope with the trauma caused by slavery. It may seem trivial for the young generation today, but it is crucial because it is one of the causes of division and suffering in Africa.

Many arrangements were made by some to ensure that their children were never captured, which constitute blockages today for their own descendants in Africa. Another thing is that certain kingdoms victimized by the capture of their children, took occult measures to preserve their people. The Vodou cast, to ensure those children's protection, is still active. It was protective measures that parents used to prevent their family from ever losing a member again. I am drawing your attention here to the irreversible, subsequent suffering that this inhuman trade inflicted on Africa. Because to this day, the continent itself is not spared the pain felt by the sons who were sold away.

This evil trade, which lasted about three hundred years, left not just scars, since no wound has been healed to this day; but rather invisible holes, a gaping void, and huge losses for Africa. She is forced to accept this reality without a way out and without any possible repair. History tells us that the traffickers came for the strongest, most capable young men and women to build their country. They stole Africa's best youth, the intelligent, wise, the adults, and people with good character. They were not just taking physically strong humans; they were also builders of society. In reality, Africa was stripped of her real engineers, her children who could have built her better. Thus, she was left with the submissive ones, dominated by the descendants of the former traders. Today, only the descendants of the former slave sellers who were dazzled and seduced by the white merchants are left. Africa has still not experienced true independence, because nothing has really changed since ancient times.

Former human traffickers, as well as sellers' descendants, still hold decision-making and influential power today. No change is possible if this continues. Did Africa let go of all her valiant children and only kept the bad guys? The corrupt, envious ones stayed, while the good ones went on to build other places instead of their own continent. Those who only thought of themselves, the selfish and the proud ones, the ones who wanted to grow rich alone, and see their brothers in pain, stayed. All Africa has left are only the ancient destroyers and their descendants.

Africa learned white folks' language. She accepted white folks' school and embraced everything the human merchants brought; but her situation remains the same. The sun rises over misery and sets on her children's tears. Most African countries lack the energy necessary to keep every household electrified. Do you know why? Because they sold the ancestor of inventor, Lewis H. Latimer; Africa is in the dark because she gave Latimer away in exchange for junk. This is just one example of the many things she lost. She really has lost so much that the new generations are struggling to get back on their feet. The evil done for three hundred years, now demands accountability. It was no coincidence that those children were born in Africa; there is a reason for everything. Africa today is the result of our ancestors' ambition and naivety which left her a legacy of dependence and admiration for everything that white folks bring her.

Africa has, as a result of what she did to her own children, been setback; the former slaves build other continents. A subsequent problem, therefore, continues to plague her and stems from slavery's victims. Many trends in Africa today actually come from the slave's lineage. Young Africans, for example, have become practically copies of African Americans youth. African youngsters wear their pants down to the bottom of the buttocks, adopt a lame and cramped gait, and wear big chains around their necks. Imitating the young African American. The same is true of haircuts, choice of shoes, glasses, dance steps, body gestures, and even the way of speaking. And this is no coincidence; this blood recognizing its coordinates from afar. African Americans' blood communicates with African blood. African youth copying its American counterpart is not just the mimicry, but the profound expression of a behavior in them, without them realizing what they are doing. African girls go so far as to put on artificial eyelashes and fake nails; they dress in American styles and wear wigs to have long hair. This is pure contamination. Neither white nor Chinese ladies wear wigs; it is rather the black ones who seek to have the hair like their masters. Some former female slaves wanted to have long hair like their mistresses back in the day also! The African market is invaded with all sorts of hair and body care products that could help them resemble the masters or mistresses of the past. This practice came from slaves who nurtured the dream of living like their masters. Some reject the black color of their skin and use chemicals to bleach it to obtain a lighter skin. These attempts bring about serious health consequences.

Africa's dream is in many ways an unrealistic one for it is based on colonial and deceitful factors. It is a dream with no fundamental reference and is in no way linked to Africa's original sources. Spiritually speaking, Africa has no religion of its own; what we have is a mixture of culture and religion. Within is a spiritual war discreetly introduced by the colonizer. The African seeks to lead a Westernized style of life when his original lifestyle is far better. A rich African sees himself as a Western man and treats those around him as he wants. He is just a copy of a European; he just does not realize it. The same applies to rich African Americans.

What has Africa done to find herself in this position? Well, she just sold her own children who would have built her to the Europeans merchants. She traded her successful future for junk. Africa today, represents nothing more than the junk she had accepted to give her brave children away.

I cannot help but ask myself, where would Africa be today if the famous African American inventors were born and raised in Africa? I can only imagine her tremendous success at any level. Africa would not be the beggar she is today, despite being very rich with all the resources she has. Yet, all she does is reach out to beg because she traded her most precious wealth for junk. One is tempted to say Africa has been cursed. Something one must acknowledge before trying to find a solution. The tragedy though, is that those who understood that and attempted to end the curse, were quickly murdered by, or in complicity with their own brothers. Mohamed Gaddafi, Thomas Sankara, Sékou Toure, Patrice Lumumba, Kwame Nkrumah, etc., were killed by their own relatives manipulated by the former merchants, or their descendants, who promised them a dream life, a westernized lifestyle.

Here is the story of a certain African President who came into power after the assassination of a great African leader. He, for the first time in his life, bathed in a pool; and later built a castle to fulfill a dream he had during his childhood. Several leaders were murdered, not by the Europeans, but by their own brothers just to serve the Western cause. An illustration of this occurred in the history of Dahomey. There was a king named Adandozan who was totally opposed to the slave trade. He was against this trade, which to him was inhumane and bad for his kingdom. He even imprisoned his brother, Guezo, who was also an heir to the royal throne. He also had his mother sold to show his people how dangerous such a trade could be to the kingdom.

By his bold act, he proved to his people that anyone could be exposed to the trauma caused by slavery. For daring to oppose slavery the way he did, King Adandozan was removed by his brother who was in prison. He did so with the help of the renowned trader, Felix Chacha Souza, established in Ouidah; especially for human trafficking business. King Adandozan was then overthrown and murdered by Guezo with the support of the European Felix Chacha Souza; and the slave trade, forbidden by the late king, resumed. We are experiencing the same thing today. Past misfortunes continue to plague Africa. The European merchants passed their deceitful tricks down to their children. The continent has not evolved, but still lives with the past evil, mainly because of the remorseless ambition descendants of slaves' sellers inherited from their parents.

It is now clear that black Africa will not see her suffering end until the slave's descendants are released spiritually and physically. The flip side of the problem: black Africa, and especially the countries that served as pillars of the slave trade, cannot experience relief and peace as long as the souls of some of her sold children cry out from the Atlantic Ocean and demand freedom.

The misfortune ruining black Africa will not come to an end until the slaves' descendants are in peace. Our ancestors in those days sold not just human beings, but the clean blood of worthy sons who could have built the continent. The problem continues in many forms; and I am an example: through my presence in this country, the United States of America, I tirelessly make physical and mental efforts to contribute in my own way, to the evolution of this society every day.

My hard work here every day could have contributed to building my own country. But Africa's problem has, since ancient times, prevented her youth from contributing effectively to her development. I may see things differently, which make some people sometimes think I am weird. But in truth, it is my way of understanding things, and drawing a conclusion in order to come up with a solution. The consequences of once selling her own blood which helped build other countries and continents for years, prevent black Africa from freeing herself from the issues she is experiencing today. These continents, continuously progressing, have become refuges for Africans who have been able to find a way out to survive, and feed their families who stayed behind.

Difficulties spread day by day and forces young people to flee the continent at the risk of perishing in deserts or oceans. This historical evil still strikes and rejects the new generation; he pushes them out of the continent. The curse strikes in all areas and literally hurt the younger generations' future. All this because of the profound evil the ancestors attracted, brought upon the continent by selling their own brothers and sisters.

Betrayal between brothers is another deplorable phenomenon. The observation is that black people almost always betray one another. He who manages to understand things and seeks to bring the continent out of misfortune, is murdered by his closest brother or friend. Nothing in life is created, everything is transformed. Africa's transformation today stems from the first interactions between the black continent and others. The betrayals also have their origin in those first interactions.

Black folks betray each other in Africa as those in the Americas also do. They kill each other in Africa as do those in America. Maybe with one difference: witchcraft kills in Africa every day, while guns are used in America.

We are alike, inhabited by pessimism; black folks remain the cause of their own misfortune. In addition, there is a negative perception of our race. Everywhere on the planet, our black skin is associated with every bad thing happening. A treatment that makes me cry for my race, one of which I remain proud; but for which I am sometimes fearful. I work to protect my race, but sometimes feel despair or reservations in my willingness to do things right; because the future tells something that I refuse to believe.

I very much want my race to understand things as they are, to build a different future. But it is as if every day offers an opportunity for my race to sink a little deeper into its shame. This obviously started a long time ago, and the problem goes back to an old root difficult to cut; trust me it is not for lack of will. Some of my ancestors have already tried to cut the root of the evil, but those who were supposed to help them, became their murderers. I believe in the God who greatly inspired me for this book. I also rely on Him to open my cousins' eyes, so they can be relieved from their current experiences.

At this point, a courageous resolution must be made. Dear Africa, acknowledge that everything that happens to you, good and ill, comes from you. Recognize that you are the source of your own misfortune. Stop blaming others and be aware of what is going on. Stop ruining your children's lives; be aware of the resources you still have in your soil. Give a clean and dignified conscience to your children, who will now be able to build you to the satisfaction of all.

CHAPTER XIV

SOURCE

When I refer to source, I take an in depth look at the root of our life. When I talk about source, I speak of a reference I can turn back to whenever I feel the need to regain my personality, my identity, and my courage. I am talking about the thing that urges me to hold on to the upbringing I received; and work hard to stay true to my values. I look at my cousins and feel a very heavy pain from the depths of my heart, like condensed water vapor in a closed pot. I get them though; the source from where everything that guarantees a better life starts simply does not exist.

Allow me to share my oldest daughter's struggle at the age of eleven. She came to America at a very young age, and after turning eleven, started showing strange behaviors. Those of a child who lost her directions. She rejected everything that originated from Africa, mainly from Benin, our country of origin. She began imitating a culture that was not her own; her behavior towards us, her parents, and other members of the larger family, changed. My wife and I, deeply concerned by what our once sweet child was going through, made the decision to go back to Benin without delay.

We knew our baby girl needed the opportunity to reconnect with her source. That place that would allow her to reconnect with the realities that made her parents well raised, respectful, and responsible people. A source which brought her father and mother together in the respect of the culture and principles of their own parents.

Believe me when I tell you that taking our child back home was a wonderful experience. Watching her carry water on her head for almost a kilometer and a half, walk three kilometers to and from school every morning and evening. It was humbling and inspiring for her to live a reality that is totally different from what she experienced in the United States. As a result, she quickly recovered from that phase she was going through.

After returning to America, she is again the sweet child appreciated by all. So, staying three years in her homeland and reconnecting with her source, were enough to pass onto her the true values of what we in Benin call "well-raised children". I share this story with you to tell you that when you do not know where you're going, you need to at least know where you come from. It was an experience that now gives us a lot of confidence about our daughter's behavior and future; allowing us to completely trust her. I once shared this happy experience with an American client who was interested in doing the same with his own boy, but he did not know where to start because he didn't know Africa. He did not know how to go about this reconnection experiment, because he has no connection to our continent. It would not be easy for him as it was for us because it is our source. From the African earth came our blood, and it easily recognizes it and replenishes it in times of hardships.

Adding to this development is the example of our younger daughter who asks to return to Africa all the time to have her own experience. She dreams of riding on a motorbike with us, drinking Bissap (a very tasty local fruit juice), walking freely in the streets, and having fun in the sand. From her first stay, at barely two-years-old, she kept a reference, an image so strong of her source, that she clearly makes the difference. This story provides proof of what I call, the source. I imagine many living in the United States of America, who like me, take the time to return to Africa, or their country of origin to recharge their batteries. They will surely bear witness to the unrivalled benefits of such an experience.

The greatest experiences I have had while writing this book, are the moments of deep meditations that I rigorously observe every morning in order to find the common thread for my writings. And mostly, rejuvenate myself with the positive energy coming from my native land, and ask the universe for the multitude of information it holds about it. This daily experience has always seemed moving and impressive to me. Strong and frequent visions come to me through my third eye. I immerse myself in real emotional moments, which allows me to better understand and demonstrate what I expose. Thus, I manage to express myself even beyond my own expectations, because the spiritual realities of this story are delivered to me in visions in a natural or sometimes even supernatural way.

At some point, it was necessary for me to get in touch with a renowned professor in Benin who is knowledgeable about the Vodou culture and the history of endogenous values. I did so as to confirm my ideas and make sure that the visions were not merely unfounded illusions. In one of his demonstrations on this chapter, the professor said that the source has been amputated, and the pieces must be reconnected before Africa and her children elsewhere can experience real peace and proper evolution. I felt a real sensation at the very moment he was talking about this, because a vision of the source had been shown to me during a meditation; here it is:

I saw a triangle of a dark greyish color demonstrated as a precious and valuable object. This triangle represented the route of the shameful Transatlantic Trade, Europe-Africa-America-Europe. During this slave trade, an angle was torn off. The African angle, the spiritual source of the homeland of a rich and fulfilled people. The triangle was normally supposed to be placed on its base emitting rays of intense light, but it has been amputated, and could no longer stand on its base.

I immediately understood that the African source is now like a broken gemstone. The mutilated triangle has become worthless in the absence of the piece that was torn from it. It can no longer stand in balance in any form. I saw myself taking the triangle in my hands and cried all the tears in my eyes. In my tears, a light visited me and illuminated from afar the amputated part, which was like in a distant desert, not cared for and dusty. I walked in one direction as if to retrieve that part of the triangle with the intention of putting the pieces back together; but the road ahead seemed very long. I had to walk several days.

It was during the walk to save the loose piece that I suddenly came back from my deep journey. I still try, every time I meditate, to go back as soon as possible; in order to collect the missing part of the triangle. But I always feel far from achieving it. I believe that the secret has been shown to me so that I work hard, not only to collect the amputated part of the triangle, but also to keep the two pieces strictly glued for all eternity. I relive this vision all the time so that it always keeps my mind awaken and determined to finish writing this book. Which to me, represents the way of recovering the amputated part of the triangular source, our common source.

The source was amputated for a reason, the slave trade. But today, neither this reason nor cooperation can put the pieces back together. The amputated part is abandoned and deteriorating in a hot desert. This small missing part is important and very indispensable to the source, to the point of creating a total imbalance to the rest of it.

You may renounce your nationality and adopt another; however, your source will forever remain the same. You can never help but think according to your source, who always holds a major part of your subconscious. The magical nature of this source is that you always belong to it without it demanding anything from you in return. Just like gravity that brings you back to earth no matter how high you reach in the sky.

A luxury car may cost thousands of dollars. After serving its purpose it ends up in a junk yard and returns to the source; that is the land productive of the raw material from which it was made. Everything that leaves the earth always comes back to it, even if in another form. The human body is the perfect illustration of matter returning to the source, the earth from which it was drawn. The source then, has a similar power that never let you lose, no matter what arrangements you make in the future; be it acquiring another nationality. Numerous Africans have become Americans; yet they still have an extraordinarily strong attachment to their homeland and their mentality will never be a purely American one.

So, one's source is full of the information one needs to grow and succeed in one's endeavors. One's source, one's origin is, therefore, a pillar that brings several necessary elements to one's life; to help one become who one wants to be. The source sometimes dictates its law depending on the cultures and traditions that influenced one early on. However, this does not prevent one from controlling one's mind in terms of organizing one's own existence, despite any plans the source could have made for one.

With regards to the African Americans, the descendants still carry the same characteristics as the main source from which they were weaned or cut. But this reference will serve them no purpose today because most of the new generation ignore it and nothing is being done to help them return.

I can't say it enough, the African American need to baptize himself, to plunge back into the source of his origin to repair this amputation and reconnect to real life. Remember, the slave did not inherit any plan or means to escape this amputation, or to prevent it from having its effect. Slavery imposed a different life method to which slaves were to submit to. The slave in the United States had no choice but to deny their origin and copy the master. The treatment might be different elsewhere. His situation in Haiti, for example, is different. A reference representing the source is present, Vodou. The practice of Vodou in Haiti and Brazil makes it easier for the descendants of former slaves in those communities to at least know their origin, even though they cannot all return. To worship the Vodou, they had to speak the language of their origin to it, and maintaining the celebratory songs directly orient them to their origin. Cult and culture have always been fundamental elements that define origin, the source.

Can we nowadays speak of a black American culture per se, if only to refer to their new lifestyle that now defines them culturally? The constant quest for a better life requires them to ignore their origin, their own source, and to adopt a style. A way of life that does not relate their existence to the realities of their source, but rather to a slave origin. This voluntary or involuntary option unfortunately does not serve their interest and can never ensure their prosperity.

Whatever their efforts, they will indeed always be deprived of the energy that must come from the source. In reality, this lack, this failure is silently imposed in the daily lives of the African Americans. The source not being involved in them, keeps the keys to the African Americans' prosperity. It retains all the data, all the energies that the young African American necessarily needs to flourish and make his life radiant. Whitney Houston is a perfect example to prove this. She had a tremendous success; she had all the money she might have dreamed of, but her life was not the one she would have wanted for herself. She did not experience true happiness, despite her fame and money. Her death was rather tragic and unglamorous. When one takes a careful look at the life of this respected singer who touched the world with her music, one can't help but wonder: what is really missing from the African Americans life? This question leads us to understand that neither silver nor gold, let alone success, will bring the desired change in my American cousins' lives. The problem is surely at the level of the source that holds a crucial element, the key to the true success whose continued absence condemns this race to perdition.

Could the church have filled this void? As an evangelist, even the institution of the church cannot be a real alternative to the reference problem facing my cousins. Whitney Houston began her singing career in a church; she certainly received training there. But she could not get what she lacked; and that should come from the source: energy, the key to total fulfillment. Many African Americans ended up like her, never reaching their ideal life. However, I pay a well-deserved tribute to this famous singer, whose much-loved voice could serve as a source of inspiration to get the disoriented youth to make healthy resolutions.

One might also wonder what is hidden in the source which prevent the African, as well as the African American, from finding the way to a peaceful and successful life. What does the source contain, that we blacks are subject to whatever is considered a plague in the world? The source's imbalance due to the small, amputated part of the triangle is so crucial; that now is the time to correct it.

The vision that keeps appearing to me of the source, is that of a dark greyish triangle unable to stand on its base, and part of which has been removed never to stick again. What a disaster! Doesn't someone's heart bleed? Doesn't someone's soul cry for what is happening in Africa and America? What are the ways and possibilities for healing this source today? How do I put the amputated piece back to the original? So many questions remained unanswered, while in Africa, the source herself, is making her complain by revolting; posing as a victim, she is claiming the portion that has been taken from her.

The profound meaning of this vision is that because of the reality we all know, it is now important to wake up Africans and African Americans alike. To first, understand the root causes of our common situation that I denounce. Secondly, to together seek and find the most appropriate ways and means to once and for all emerge from this misfortune. To guarantee our future generations a prosperous and radiant future just as all other races have.

It is now clear then, that our only salvation in such a hostile universe is in the reconnection to the primary source. The reconstruction of our entity, reconciliation and reunion between us, forgiveness, and finally, unity which is the strength of the weak. It is going to be a journey, a process that might be long, but it remains achievable thanks to goodwill that must exist and be strengthened on both sides. This is a vibrant and historic appeal that I courageously make to all parties.

CHAPTER XV

A BETTER LIFE

The Gospel Roots Program, initiated by the Late President Mathieu KEREKOU of Benin (West Africa), followed the first reconciliation and development conference in December 1999. It was supposed to allow the victims of the slave trade to recharge their batteries, to erase the pains of the past through Gospel music; and to consider forgiveness and reconciliation with the slave descendants' source. This program, which no longer exists today, was discontinued for several reasons. This leads me to say that it is not yet time to consider a significant return of the children of the former slaves. I say this because the past's wounds are still having an effect and the descendants are not yet ready to see a future on the land of their ancestors. It has been a little over three centuries; several parameters should be implemented to provide a final solution to what my African American cousins are going through. We, representing the former sellers, must accept our position in this situation and acknowledge the abuse that has been afflicted. We must do so to reassure our cousins who has been in perdition since this trade was initiated. The question from the beginning of this book was, why are African Americans in such a situation? We now understand through this book, that there is more than a problem to solve. Today, I am appeased for having been able to suggest some final resolution points to the complications in my cousins' lives.

Education in the African American History context:

We cannot continue keeping quiet about slavery and leave future generations in ignorance. Those who know their history can take initiatives to find out the origin of their problems and solve them. Museums alone are not enough to keep black children informed about their history. The internet is not enough to inform and teach black children of their ancestors' experiences. It is, therefore, particularly important to shed light on the history of the slaves who gave a lot to the United States. A special program on African American history must be designed and approved by the government so it can be taught starting in elementary schools. The slave's descendants ought to be given the value and recognition they deserve, and which really allow them to know the path to choose.

When I speak of education, I mean the work that must be offered to the descendants of slaves to break out of the mentality of limitation, by better understanding the faults committed by some ancestors. Educate them to erase the lack of self-confidence in them; take away the spirit of imitating the master and having a real personality. Does school really represent the solution my Afro-American cousins need to remedy certain afflictions? Does school really guarantee them a future without the stains of the past? Does the educational program consider the future of African Americans? Only those who can afford the tuition go to college; this can be proven by the number of the children who drop out after high school. How can the children achieve high productivity if they only have a high school diploma nowadays? Colleges are expensive; not many of my cousins are able to save for their children's university tuition. This is because not many African Americans have a job good enough to allow them to pay for their children's college courses. On the streets of Washington, D.C., they are traffic control agents. Rain or shine, they are forced to face the climate to make a living because they could not get a college education.

In the mornings, they ride behind big garbage trucks to keep the city clean through garbage collection. Someone must do it, but the number of black people doing these kinds of jobs is incomparably high. That number would be lower if young black children were given more educational opportunities and university doors were open for most of them. The chains of limitations worn by the slaves, which prevented them to go further than their master's house, still exist. My American cousins' education is limited by the high college tuition displayed in their mind. Not everyone can be eligible for the financial plans these universities offer on selection and other difficult criteria. The educational program must be revisited on two levels:

1) Establish a program which will facilitate education for African Americans in specific areas and get them interested in going to school. A great emphasis should be put on their history. Define encouraging and motivating references that give them proof that their future will be better through their education.

2) The loosening up policies which governs universities, to allow many African Americans access to a college education.

An effort must be made by the American government, as well as the wealthy black people who should be the first to care about their future generations. This to me is important even though it has nothing to do with the spiritual. This book is mostly about the spiritual, and most of the solutions it offers are spiritual; but a reliable education will also support the liberation of a source of misfortune.

Reconciliation:

We, Africans, African Americans, or descendants of black slaves, must all meet somewhere in the world, around a table of peace and reconciliation. Black people living outside of Africa look at it from afar and feel like undesired Africans from the depths of their hearts. This does not encourage them to travel to Africa. It is imperative to find, again and again, any necessary means for a remarkable reconciliation, despite the efforts that have already been made. Africa must acknowledge the harm done to her children. The African countries must take things seriously regarding their children, who left a little over three centuries ago. They must not simply limit themselves to what has done by presidents who understood that African Americans and black folks everywhere else are Africa's treasures.

Africa finds herself in this situation today because she gave her own many treasures to other continents. Africa must reach out to them by expressing great regret over the acts of the past and sincere requests for forgiveness. Africa must woo her children today and give them what is rightfully theirs: respect, trust, love, culture, identity, and the land of their ancestors. Today, it is necessary to establish a remarkably close trust of good morality, of honesty.

Africa must take off her old trading mask and design a plan with a pure spirit of final reconciliation. No one is going to do it for her. Look at great inventors like Lewis Howard Latimer, who developed the light bulb. He was a descendant of those whom Africa sold, and part of her is still in the dark; the people still use oil lanterns. This is an example of how much Africa lost.

We need to understand that part of Africa's value is elsewhere, and that she herself gave it away at a cheap price. Reconciliation calls upon us all and requires many other steps that must start from the source of history to be effective. The history of African American slavery should no longer be taken as history belonging in museums. It must now be a reference for reparation and healing for not only the slaves' descendants, but also a change of mentality for the sellers' descendants. The buyers' descendants will not do it for us. If this were in their interest, much reparation would have come from former slaves' buyers and owners regarding Africa and her children. Reconciliation in all aspects, reconciliation of descendants with their source and culture, reconciliation with great decisions for change.

Forgiveness:

There will never be reconciliation without forgiveness. In this case, true forgiveness will come from the side of the slave descendants. It is important for all to leave this heavy past behind to overcome evil, a past that hurts from generation to generation. A new door must be opened to the spirit for liberation through forgiveness. Most of the children who had the opportunity to visit the land of their ancestors and followed in their footsteps through the slave route, get angry. Today, we want to remove the veils on all that was hidden about the slave trade. We want to lead all slave descendants, from all over the world, to understand the past, so as to build the future differently. The request for forgiveness coming from Africa must be accepted by those who remain victims of this sad trafficking.

Africa's forgiveness request must bring value to all her children on the continent and, above all, an assurance of regret. This request needs to be accepted because no spiritual healing will take place amid divergence and weeping. Forgiveness must regenerate the hearts of all for it to bring energy for the remaining of the steps to be taken to end African Americans' suffering. I cry in silence for my African American cousins whose bodies and souls hurt. At the same time, I kneel before them to ask for a deep forgiveness; because my eyes have seen the disturbing realities which they face daily. Africa must ask forgiveness for herself, question herself, and know that somewhere in the world her children's souls cry out for revenge.

Forgiveness will appease the souls of those who were thrown into the ocean and never made it to the Europeans' land. Forgiveness will appease the souls of those buried in mass graves because they couldn't take the treatment they were submitted to before boarding. The souls of those killed cold bloodedly by the Europeans; the souls of those tortured to death, the souls of those who were raped, the souls of the mothers who lived in the pain of the capture of their husbands and children. They will all be appeased when forgiveness is symbolically requested and accepted.

Forgiveness will give us a path of spiritual solution because spirits will now be in favor of the development of the black race around the world. The forgiveness request will not only come from Africa. Other parties also involved in this are descendants of former slave traders and owners. They are also expected to request forgiveness. Therefore, I see the Museum of African American History in Washington, D.C., initiated by President George Bush and inaugurated by President Baraka OBAMA on September 28, 2016, as a symbol of recognition for African Americans. The Europeans who needed the black race to build their countries should issue a request for forgiveness. It is important that African Americans also do not focus too much on this aspect, but also symbolically accept what is in order to move beyond their current situation.

Religions:

Most religions nowadays are large conviction enterprises regarding the people they lead; and they cannot be forgotten in these solutions that we seek on both sides. Most African Americans are Christians, which calls for the systematic intervention of churches in the life-changing program for my cousins. The religious work to be done is now psychological, and it will no longer be enough to just preach the Bible. Churches will have to spread the word from the source of history to bring the cousins to reason. *"In the beginning was the word, and the word was with God, the word was God, and nothing was done without it."* (John 1:1). We need that word to rebuild; we need it to lift the afflicted, the lame; we need it to restore hope, confidence, and encouragement. It is necessary today to engage with the churches with the goal to better African Americans' lives. Churches are already present and working with the children whose orientation we want to change. These churches must offer programs which can attract more of those who are lost and scattered in order to give them love; to give them hope.

Whitney Houston's dream when she was a little girl was to become a choir member like her mother and her wish was fulfilled. That is where, according to Wikipedia, that she learned her trade as a singer. The way I see it, that starting point was the best possible support the famous singer needed to succeed in her life. But she went on, despite her wealth and the bodyguards, to collapse like the Titanic in the ocean, dragging her daughter in her path. I look back at this talented woman's journey, her marriage, the suffering that made her turn to drugs, only to become a rich ruin with no future.

Money only follows one's fate. Money's energy sniffs the blood to know its direction once one has received it. That is why many people work yet have nothing to show for the money they earn. You can work for the same company trading in hours of work, earning the same salary at the end of each week, and never achieve the same goal. The flow of money depends on the fate following us from childhood or from our life's star. Therefore, many wealthy African Americans face problems and have a sad end. They are faced with an inner life battle between bondage and wealth.

Had the pastor leading Whitney's Baptist church invested more in the deep spiritual and sought to know a little more about the future of his spiritual children. Had the church understood back then what I am unveiling today. Had Whitney's parents, and herself, understood that there was a curse to be broken; her story would have been different. The African American church ignores these parameters, in my opinion. If Whitney Houston would have understood the curse of slavery, then she would certainly have invested some of her wealth to undo it. Someone could have been able to inform her of the issue, of the spiritual virus that has been without a cure for ages. The African American church needs to know about the ongoing curse, that there is work that must be done. They must investigate and wake up from their spiritual slumber. To not only stop giving hope indefinitely to the children, but also to work for their spiritual liberation.

I am not just addressing Christian churches. There are other religions with African American members. The latter are silently suffering deep within themselves. It is time for these religions also to wake up and understand that in addition to their doctrine, they owe it to their members to help them find happiness and inner peace. To help them truly live by fulfilling their desires and dreams. All religions embraced by my cousins are to use their power to act positively for a reassuring hope. We need change, and this is what we demand via this book of all religions, despite their doctrine.

To end my cousins' suffering everyone must get onboard with this reconstruction plan.

Deliverance:

To my knowledge as an Evangelist, when we speak of a curse, no final liberation happens without deliverance taking place beforehand. The deliverance, in this context, must take place in majority of the African American populations' lives, rich as well as poor. Deliverance will bring an opening to the blood, the soul, in such a way that the African Americans will find their path not only spiritually, but also physically.

Even the world leaders sometimes need it to break the old alliance in their lives and have a new beginning for a better future. During the preparations for my ordination, I found myself faced with realities forcing me to undergo a deliverance; not because of a hold, but to break a spiritual chain that went against my commitment to the position that I was going to religiously occupy. It was a great experience during which I found myself in unprecedented settings.

Many people think of possession by a spirit when talking about deliverance and are skeptical. The deliverance can be done to cancel a blockage, break a chain, undo a family curse, etc. In this case, I propose specific kinds of deliverance to achieve important results:

1) Deliverance of the blood (the soul):

This will consist of cleaning the blood of all properties and denomination that have defined the African Americans as slaves in the invisible world. The deliverance of the blood will be the liberation of the soul from the hold, that for some time, has been explicitly defining the slave descendants' fate. This operation will target the source of birth and the future of the slave descendants by completely denying their ancestors fate and officially claiming their true liberation. It will be the largest deliverance, the most important one too. For this event, pastors, evangelists, exorcist priests, and other experts in the field, will be needed. We will not only face the grip of slavery's curse; but also prepare for other strongholds that would have taken up residence in the same blood. This is not an easy task; these souls have for a long time nurtured the spirits, legions who have settled in the lives of the children to be delivered. I am convinced that this operation will succeed because every knee shall bow down before the holy name of Christ.

2) Deliverance of the name:

This consists of erasing the harmful effects of the past serial numbers and slave names which were given to the ancestors; and which could define their disorientation. We need to spiritually rethink the names, Tetragrammic values, and find the key to the names that could help prosper. The name of a person, as I said in a previous chapter, also defines him. So, the liberation of my African Americans cousins from the evil effects of the names attributed to their forefathers is important. It all comes down to understanding what it is all about and accepting it for a better future.

Mandatory deliverance before marriage:

I always recommend couples who come to my office for advice regarding their marriage, individual deliverance before getting married; and doing so if they are already married. This is not only for the well-being of their life as a couple, but for their home, as well as for the fruit of the womb. Curses or alliances differ from a family to another. Many couples separate not because they do not love each other or no longer have the will to live together. There are several parameters that push them to a divorce. Deliverance may be needed even if one is not possessed by a demon, like I said earlier.

The deliverance before marriage for my Afro-American cousins will give them the assurance that the man will stay and take responsibility as a husband and father for the rest of his days. The woman will be a married woman, the crown her man needs. We today, will say no to divorce or any other thing that mess African American children's upbringing and education up from an early age by separating the family. Through deliverance, we will say no to the separation of black families as it was done in ancestral times. This deliverance will allow us to build very strong and happy African American families from now on. It will help us clean up the curses of selling and buying the African American child.

Recharge:

It will be good if at least every African American had the opportunity to set foot on his ancestral land. Though this is possible, it will require a great organization. I believe in organizing a spiritual reload ceremony so as my cousins' souls could taste the flavor of their ancestral land. This ceremony must be profoundly spiritual in order to attract Africa's energy to quench the cousins' thirst for their origin. I would also suggest hypnosis meditations which will make the subconscious travel to the promised land, stories of the ancient people. Having special classes in this framework that will give these children comforting ideas of their origin. Marriage between Africans and Afro-Americans would be a way of charging at the original source.

Physical-spiritual treatment:

I could not highlight the parameters of the afflictions undermining African Americans without really coming up with a personal solution drawn from my spiritual art. I had the courage and audacity to write this book, considering how very reactive and bitter my cousins can be when it comes to talking about their lives. This is because I have great tools that can definitely help them overcome everything they've been through. I will not limit myself to the general various solutions I mentioned earlier knowing well that everyone could propose a solution. The singularity here is that I bring something more to the table, assets to help my cousins. I have tools which I can highlight in my cousins' lives to give back to this land of the United States that welcomed me a few years ago. I have already had the opportunity to heal, restore many people through my spiritual program, and many benefits from my spiritual works. Through my program, *"Giveback America* GBA", with great compassion and determination to help African Americans end hardships in their lives, I will make myself available to my African American cousins who would decide to change their lives. Since I have always seen this book as a solution, I will proudly open the spiritual door, which was closed in my cousins' lives. I will show the light to follow so the slave ancestors rest in peace. Martin Luther King Jr., Malcolm X, and all those who shed their blood for my cousins' healing and liberation, will rejoice in heaven if they have not reincarnated yet. Today, I am filled with pride, not out of pride, but rather out of enthusiasm to see a spiritual solution in the Afro-Americans' lives.

Let me give an overview of this program in three main points:

Psychotherapy:

In Pranic Healing, it is one of the sensitive and quick practices to cure diseases of any kind. Psychotherapy consists of fetching the elements on the protective web of the various energy centers of the body, to free the patient from the grip they have on him. So, this therapy is going to play a huge detoxification role with the smokers, alcoholics, the derailed ones. It will also help them be confident. Psychotherapy really will be the quickest modus operandi after bringing the subconscious back to normal and giving it new guidance information. It will be very essential in this program in liberating the cousins' mind and self-confidence.

The re-reading of life:

This is also a great spiritual therapy allowing to see the past life of the individual, his karmic values. Then, proceed to a cancellation of the karma little by little. It will, moreover, give a direction in the choice of life one wants to lead, a guidance about the feasibility of the choice. Re-reading can also allow us to see a child's future and take measures to secure it by moving away from all kinds of bundles of destruction.

The discovery of one true self:

Most of us today are what the system in place wants us to be. We reflect our parents' fear, lack of trust and confidence. We are the product of lousy plans, negative words, dictatorship of our parents, friends, and sometimes educators. I suggest today that everyone, especially African Americans, reconnect with their inner being which is the essence of who they truly are and allow themselves to have confidence in themselves. To truly be the image of who they need to be. This program defines inner identity; it can be relied on to open life's petals and keep them connected to an inexhaustible source for a prosperous life. Discovering one true self is not just for African Americans; it is a rich program for anyone wishing to truly walk into his destiny. It offers the opportunity to discover one's true character, and above all, to have all the tools necessary to face life's obstacles.

CONCLUSION

My book ends on the hopeful note of seeing the new African American generation fly freely and promptly like the eagle. My heart is filled with hope rooted in my faith. This is a new beginning, and this book is the start of a new era of regeneration for my African American cousins. I rejoice for coming to terms with my ideas of giving African Americans hope and conveying the message of re-building their life. I am at peace with myself and proud to discover myself as a solution author. This book was not written for any kind of personal glory. My goal is to act as a generator of solutions to spiritual liberation for my sisters and brothers in hopes they would seek freedom in my words.

I could not have written this book without divine guidance. I could not have finished it without the angels' support. I remember those moments during which I felt blockages to lay my visions bare; the headaches I had every time I had to tell this spiritual truth. The fevers that suddenly invaded me because I wanted to reveal some shocking truths. The fear that came over me in a vision of the day after the publication of this book. I believe and know that divine and pure support enlightens my visions and especially my life as an innocent young man. I reached the destination and feel relieved. I am ready to put myself at the service of the divine reiterating my fidelity, my availability, and my respect as always for the liberation of spirits still behind the wall.

References

*Note: Most of the research was conducted in French, which gives us several references (books, manuscripts, websites) in French. The websites can be translated into English, if needed. And as far as the books are concerned, some do not have an English version.

Books

Le Royaume d'Abomey Histoire et Ses Rois (The Kingdom of Abomey History and Its Kings)

Author: Christian Dedet

Pages: 291

Editor: Actes Sud (3 février 2000)

Collection: Aventure

Language: French

ISBN-10: 2742725415

ISBN-13: 9782742725410

Cultes Vodoun et Textes Oraux des Wéménou du sud Bénin (Voodoo Cults and Oral Texts of the Wéménou of southern Benin)

LW/T 19: Cultes Vodoun et Textes Oraux des Wéménou du sud Bénin (e-book)

Author: Roger Brand

Languages of the World/Text Collections 19. 100pp. 2000.

ISBN-13: 9783895866852 (print)

ISBN-13: 9783862889549 (e-book, pdf)

Route de l'Esclave (Slave Route)

- Conference de lancement de la route de l'Esclave. UNESCO,

- La chaine et le lien: une vision de la traite negriere (D. Diene ED) ED UNESCO

La traite négrière Ouida (The Ouidah slave trade)

Ouidah: The Social History of a West African Slaving Port, 1727–1892

Auteur: Robin Law

Series: Western African Studies

Paperback: 320 pages

Publisher: James Currey; UK ed. edition (November 9, 2004) -

Language: English

ISBN-10: 0852554974

ISBN-13: 978-0852554975

L'arbre Fétiche (The Fetish Tree)

Author: Jean Pliya

EAN: 9782723500074

Editor: HACHETTE (30/11/-1)

The Power Of I Am

Originally published: October 6, 2015

Author: Joel Osteen

Genres: Self-help book, Christian literature

(The American Sociology of Poverty, from the Wilsonian Ghetto to the Global City)

La sociologie américaine de la pauvreté, du ghetto wilsonien à la ville globale

Clément Théry et François Bonnet Dans Sociologie 2016/1 (Vol. 7), pages 77 à 94

Holy Bible KJV / Louis Second

- 1 Corinthians 2: 10 – 14

- Mathieux 5: 13 – 14

- Genesis: 37

- Exodus: 2

- Genesis 17: 1 – 5, 15

- Genesis 32: 25 – 29

Websites

Geography of Republic of Benin

- Wikipedia, the free encyclopedia:

https://en.wikipedia.org/wiki/Benin
https://en.wikipedia.org/wiki/History_of_the_Kingdom_of_Dahomey

- Nations online:

https://www.nationsonline.org/oneworld/benin.htm

- Wikipedia, the free encyclopedia:

https://en.wikipedia.org/wiki/History_of_the_Kingdom_of_Dahomey

- **Wikipedia, the free encyclopedia:**

https://en.wikipedia.org/wiki/Ouidah

Anne Urbanowski:

https://doi.org/10.4000/orda.1668

1968 Etats-Unis: Quarante ans après le rapport Kerner: progrès et contrastes (Forty years after the Kerner Report: progress and contrasts)

La « Route de l'esclave » de Ouidah (Bénin): espace de négociation des mémoires collectives des traites négrières et de l'esclavage. (The "Slave Route" of Ouidah (Benin): space for negotiation of collective memories of the slave trade and slavery.)

Rossila GOUSSANOU, doctorante (Université de Nantes/ENSA Nantes, UMR AAU/Equipe CRENAU) https://hal.archives-ouvertes.fr/hal-01826345/document (french)

Nipsey Hussle

Wikipedia, the free encyclopedia:

https://en.wikipedia.org/wiki/Nipsey_Hussle

Malcolm X

Wikipedia, the free encyclopedia:

https://en.wikipedia.org/wiki/Malcolm_X

https://en.wikipedia.org/wiki/Thomas_Hagan

Civil rights movement

Wikipedia, the free encyclopedia:

https://en.wikipedia.org/wiki/Civil_rights_movement   (English) https://fr.wikipedia.org/wiki/Mouvement_afro-am%C3%A9ricain_des_droits_civiques (French)

Ku Klux Klan

Wikipedia, the free encyclopedia:

https://en.wikipedia.org/wiki/Ku_Klux_Klan

https://www.history.com/topics/reconstruction/ku-klux-klan

Black Pass

https://www.blackpast.org/african-american-history/inkwell-martha-s-vineyard-1890s/

George Washington Carver

Wikipedia, the free encyclopedia:

https://en.wikipedia.org/wiki/George_Washington_Carver

Washington Post Staff July 26, 2016: Transcript: Read Michelle Obama's full speech from the 2016 DNC

https://www.washingtonpost.com/news/post-politics/wp/2016/07/26/transcript-read-michelle-obamas-full-speech-from-the-2016-dnc/

George Stinney

WIS NEWS 2014: Murder case of SC's youngest execution to be revisited
https://www.wistv.com/story/24500466/murder-case-of-scs-youngest-execution-to-be-revisited/?autostart=true

Washington Post Dec. 18, 2014: By Lindsey Bever (Reporter) It took 10 minutes to convict 14-year-old George Stinney Jr. It took 70 years after his execution to exonerate him.

https://www.washingtonpost.com/news/morning-mix/wp/2014/12/18/the-rush-job-conviction-of-14-year-old-george-stinney-exonerated-70-years-after-execution/

Segregation

Jim Crow Law

https://www.nofi.media/2017/02/jim-crow/35768

From Slavery to Segregation

https://segregationinamerica.eji.org/report/from-slavery-to-segregation.html

Liberia, le retour ratee des afro-descendants (Liberia, the failed return of Afro-descendants)

https://www.lisapoyakama.org/liberia-le-retour-rate-des-afrodescendants/

Des Afro-américains de retour en Afrique (African Americans returning to Africa)

https://www.un.org/africarenewal/fr/magazine/ao%C3%BBt-2015/des-afro-am%C3%A9ricains-de-retour-en-afrique (French)

Retour sur l'histoire de la Gold Coast au Ghana (Back to the history of the Gold Coast in Ghana)

https://www.le-voyage-autrement.com/ghana/mag/retour-sur-l-histoire-de-la-gold-coast (French)

Others

Les mille couleurs des femmes (The thousand colors of women)

https://www.univ-lyon3.fr/retour-sur-les-mille-couleurs-des-femmes-l-antre-d-adidjaly-lecture-theatrale-2 (French)

Les dates clés de l'Histoire de l'esclavage pratiqué par la France (The key dates in the history of slavery practiced by France)

https://www.jeuneafrique.com/433230/societe/chronologie-dates-cles-de-lhistoire-de-lesclavage-france/ (French)

The knife, being an instrument in the hands of men; only the one holding it decides what to do with it. We can't qualify or say Vodou is negative. But let's hold accountable the master of the Vodou to define what this one is choosing to do with it. Of course, it could only be for good or bad.

Evg Lael Newlife

www.ingramcontent.com/pod-product-compliance
Lightning Source LLC
Chambersburg PA
CBHW070317240426
43661CB00057B/2670